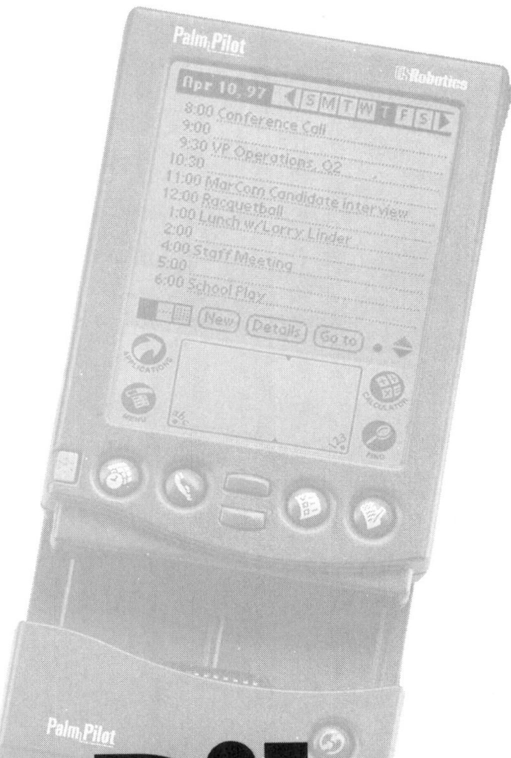

PalmPilot COMPANION

que®

PalmPilot COMPANION

que®

Steve M. Schafer

PalmPilot Companion

Library of Congress Catalog No.: 97-68098

ISBN: 0-7897-1248-2

99 98 97 6 5 4 3 2 1

Interpretation of the printing code: the rightmost double-digit number is the year of the book's printing; the rightmost single-digit number, the number of the book's printing. For example, a printing code of 97-1 shows that the first printing of the book occurred in 1997.

Screen reproductions in this book were created using Collage Plus from Inner Media, Inc., Hollis, NH.

Foreword

When we started work on the PalmPilot 3 years ago, our goal was to create the first handheld computer that people loved to carry with them everywhere. Our experience with the PDAs and handhelds that preceded PalmPilot taught us that success in this market hinged upon our ability to make a product that enabled users to accomplish specific tasks quickly and efficiently.

Of course, we had to find out what those tasks were and build a product around those demands. Our research led us to clear conclusions that the right product needed to be small, fast, easy to use, affordable, and have seamless connectivity to a desktop PC. And while that sounds like a basic formula, the development team had to constantly refine their focus to make certain that we delivered a handheld computer that met all of the criteria.

To really give people a complete experience, we also had to make sure that developers could generate solutions that take advantage of PalmPilot's portability and desktop connectivity to meet other user needs. To that end, we've built an open platform, complete with Windows and Mac development tools, and a host of resources for creating software.

Many software developers have taken advantage of this platform to build great applications that extend the functionality of the PalmPilot, from business and productivity software, to pocket versions of arcade games and puzzles. I urge you to try the compilation of software found on the CD at the end of this book, and find out how far our connected organizer can take you.

Jeff Hawkins

Founder and Vice President
Advanced Development of Palm Computing, Inc.,
a wholly owned subsidiary of 3Com Corporation

August, 1997

Table of Contents

Credits

PRESIDENT
Roland Elgey

SENIOR VICE PRESIDENT/ PUBLISHING
Don Fowley

PUBLISHER
Stacy Hiquet

GENERAL MANAGER
Joe Muldoon

MANAGER OF PUBLISHING OPERATIONS
Linda H. Buehler

PUBLISHING MANAGER
Tim Ryan

MANAGING EDITOR
Patrick Kanouse

DIRECTOR OF ACQUISITIONS
Cheryl D. Willoughby

ACQUISITIONS EDITOR
Todd Pfeffer

PRODUCT DIRECTOR
Jacquelyn Mosley Eley

PRODUCTION EDITOR
William F. McManus

PRODUCT MARKETING MANAGER
Kourtnaye Sturgeon

ASSISTANT PRODUCT MARKETING MANAGER
Gretchen Schlesinger

TECHNICAL EDITOR
Stephen L. Miller

SOFTWARE SPECIALIST
Adam Swetnam

SOFTWARE RELATIONS COORDINATOR
Susan D. Gallagher

SOFTWARE COORDINATOR
Andrea Duvall

EDITORIAL ASSISTANTS
Jennifer L. Chisholm
Travis Bartlett

BOOK DESIGNER
Ruth Harvey

COVER DESIGNER
Dan Armstrong

PRODUCTION TEAM
Melissa Coffey
Erin Danielson
Julie Geeting
Tony McDonald
Timothy Neville

INDEXER
Nick Schroeder

Composed in *Century Old Style* and *ITC Franklin Gothic* by Que Corporation.

To my one and only Angie, for continually helping me be all that I can.

About the Author

Steve Schafer is a freelance author and computer consultant. He has contributed to many Que books and has authored several books for BradyGames. When he isn't busy solving other people's technical problems, he spends time with his computer or PalmPilot, creating his own problems.

Steve can be reached on the Internet at **sschafer-pb@ synergy-tech.com**.

Acknowledgments

As with any book, this was a team project that wouldn't have been completed without the dedicated help of several individuals. In particular I'd like to thank Jim Minatel for the original concept, Todd Pfeffer for believing I could do this, Tim Ryan for continuing to manage the process and the relationship with 3Com, Jàcquie Eley for keeping me organized and on track, Steve Miller for double-checking my technical proficiency, and especially Bill McManus for making it look like I have a grasp of the English language.

Kudos also go out to the Design and Production departments at Macmillan for making it all look like a book, and a good looking one at that. Ruth Harvey, in particular, created a design specifically for this book—thanks, Ruth!

Of course, without the folks at 3Com, none of this would be possible. Thanks for making such a great product and being dedicated to constantly improving it.

Last, but certainly not least, many thanks to all the third-party developers who donate their software for the betterment of PalmPilot users everywhere.

We'd Like to Hear from You!

As part of our continuing effort to produce books of the highest possible quality, Que would like to hear your comments. To stay competitive, we *really* want you, as a computer book reader and user, to let us know what you like or dislike most about this book or other Que products.

You can mail comments, ideas, or suggestions for improving future editions to the address below, or send us a fax at (317) 581-4663. For the online inclined, Macmillan Computer Publishing has a forum on CompuServe (type **GO QUEBOOKS** at any prompt) through which our staff and authors are available for questions and comments. The address of our Internet site is **http://www.mcp.com** (World Wide Web).

In addition to exploring our forum, please feel free to contact me personally to discuss your opinions of this book: I'm **jeley@que.mcp.com** on the Internet.

Thanks in advance—your comments will help us to continue publishing the best books available on computer topics in today's market.

Jacquelyn Mosley Eley
Product Development Specialist
Que Corporation
201 W. 103rd Street
Indianapolis, Indiana 46290
USA

Introduction

On January 29, 1996, U.S. Robotics announced the "Pilot 1000," a small handheld computer. The Pilot 1000 was an instant hit upon its availability in the retail market, due to its size, innovative design, and capability to use add-on software.

The Pilot 1000 was designed to be a basic paper-organizer replacement. Its small size is the primary reason that it attained instant popularity. However, its continuing popularity and increasing sales growth are due to the ease with which its capabilities can be expanded.

In April 1997, two new models were released, the PalmPilot Personal Edition and PalmPilot Professional Edition. PalmPilot sales remain high, despite the recent release of several Windows CE Personal Digital Assistants (PDA), such as Casio's *Cassiopeia*.

Recently, CNN reported the PalmPilot accounts for up to 20 percent of *all* handheld electronic devices purchased, and has as much as 70 percent market share, with over 1 million units sold in the last two years.

What Is the PalmPilot?

At its most basic level, the PalmPilot is an electronic organizer. It offers a Date Book, Address Book, To Do List, Memo Pad, and Calculator—rivaling any "Franklin Day Planner-type" paper organizer. In fact, Franklin Quest sells a PalmPilot version of its popular planner system bundled with ascend 97 software.

PalmPilot comes with a decking cradle that attaches to a PC or Mac for transferring data to and from your computer and the PalmPilot. Desktop software that mirrors the PalmPilot's capabilities is included as well, which allows you to edit or create the data on your computer and then transfer it back to the PalmPilot.

The new PalmPilot Professional adds TCP/IP and e-mail connectivity, through the cradle or through a connection to an external modem.

The PalmPilot was not designed as a portable computing solution, but as a Personal Digital Assistant. In fact, the main draw to the PalmPilot is its simplicity—the capability to keep you organized and on time while fitting in a shirt pocket.

Additional PalmPilot Software

The PalmPilot was developed around a fairly open standard. Shortly after the Pilot 1000 was released a Software Development Kit was released to provide third-party developers the chance to create new applications for the Pilot 1000. Almost immediately, several third-party applications appeared on the Internet. Although initial applications were limited in scope, it didn't take long for developers to populate almost every software genre on the Pilot 1000.

Applications that are now available can fill the small voids in the PalmPilot's personal information and organization features, provide connectivity to popular PC and Mac applications, supply entertainment, and add to the capabilities of the basic PalmPilot design.

This Book

This book's main focus is the add-on PalmPilot software. We examined the list of available add-on PalmPilot software and then performed online research to find out generally how much each application is used and what people are saying about each application. The results of this research helped us choose the applications that are included on this book's companion CD.

This book is for anyone who wants to get the most out of their PalmPilot. The chapters of this book are task-based, organized by what you can do with your PalmPilot. Sections focused on applicable add-on software are interspersed within each chapter. An appendix is included that rounds up all the software discussed throughout the book.

This book's chapters are organized as follows:

Chapter 1, "PalmPilot Basics," explains the differences between the various PalmPilot models and offers some general tips and techniques for getting the most out of the basic PalmPilot applications.

Chapter 2, "Staying On Time," provides information about how to use the PalmPilot to maintain your schedule, remind you of important dates, and track important projects.

Chapter 3, "Staying Organized," covers how to keep your life organized by keeping your PalmPilot information organized.

Chapter 4, "Staying Informed," shows how to compile and store massive information on your PalmPilot—whether you are using Graffiti to enter the information or importing it from your PC or Mac.

Chapter 5, "Staying On Top of Finances," shows you how to step outside the boundaries of the Calculator and use the PalmPilot to track your expenses, and even balance your checkbook.

Chapter 6, "Staying Connected," explains the ins and outs of connecting your PalmPilot to your PC or Mac to translate and transfer data between your desktop and other applications, as well as tools and techniques for communicating outside of your PalmPilot.

Chapter 7, "Staying Entertained," covers all the entertainment software available for the PalmPilot—such as classic board and arcade games.

Chapter 8, "System Enhancements," is your guide to the upgrades available for the PalmPilot, as well as available third-party PalmPilot applications that increase its capabilities.

Chapter 9, "Developing PalmPilot Software," introduces the tools you can use to create your own PalmPilot applications.

Appendix A, "PalmPilot Resources," provides additional resources for PalmPilot support, add-on applications, and accessories.

Appendix B, "Software Compendium," details where you can find the software discussed in this book.

Conventions Used in This Book

Within each chapter, you will find italicized text, bulleted lists, and numbered lists. *Italics* are used to mark important words or phrases and to introduce new technical terms. An italicized term is followed by a definition or an explanation.

Bulleted lists are used when the order of the items isn't important. The items represent related concepts that are explained in the list.

Numbered lists are used when the numbering, or sequence, is important. Steps in a procedure appear in numbered lists. Follow the steps from beginning to end. Make sure that you understand each step—don't just skip one because you don't understand it.

The chapters also contain figures (which often are screen shots that show you what to expect on your PalmPilot) and code listings (which contain complete programs to illustrate a technique).

Code fragments that are contained in the text are set in `monospace` font. These fragments illustrate a technique but are not, by themselves, a complete program.

Sometimes a line runs beyond the page width of this book in these code listings. When this happens, you will see a small arrow, ➥, at the beginning of the new line. When you see this arrow, it means that all of this material can actually be entered into the program on a single line.

Characters that you are asked to type are set in **bold** font. If you must substitute a file name or other element into the line, a placeholder for the file name or element is used and is set in ***bold italics***.

The syntax of a particular command or tag is shown with a special kind of code fragment. A syntax form looks similar to the following example:

```
<P [ALIGN=Left¦Center¦Right]>
```

Here, optional elements appear in [square brackets]. Variants are separated by the vertical bar ¦. Monospaced font must be typed exactly as it appears. According to the preceding syntax form, all of the following HTML is acceptable:

```
<P>
<P ALIGN=Left>
<P ALIGN=Center>
<P ALIGN=Right>
```

and the following HTML is unacceptable:

```
<P ALIGN=Center
<P ALIGN=CenterRight>
<P COLOR="#110000">
```

Tables are used when appropriate.

Different icons appear in the page margins to indicate that a file or application exists on this book's companion CD-ROM or that an Internet address appears within the adjacent text.

CHAPTER 1

PalmPilot Basics

Now that you have purchased a PalmPilot, you will certainly what to optimize its use by learning all the tricks and techniques that will make you a more efficient PalmPilot user. Toward that goal, this chapter covers the PalmPilot hardware and some basic habits you can adopt to get the most out of your investment.

NOTE See subsequent chapters for examples of third-party software that you can use with your PalmPilot.

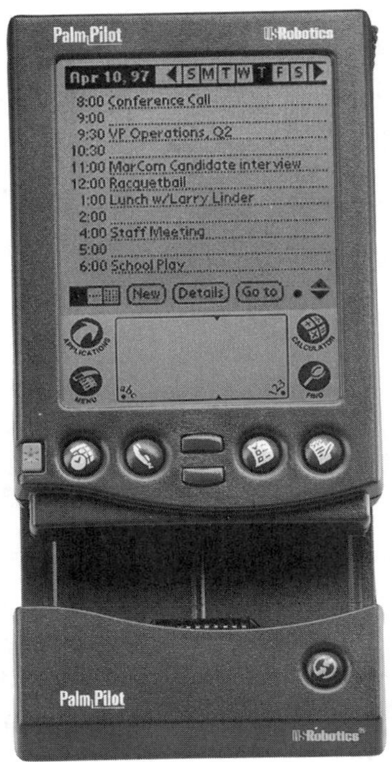

FIGURE 1.1
The PalmPilot Personal Data Assistant (PDA).

Inside the PalmPilot

The PalmPilot measures a mere 3.2 inches wide by 4.7 inches tall and 0.7 inches thick—scarcely larger than a pack of cigarettes. It weighs 5.7 ounces, including the two AAA batteries used to power the Motorola MC68328 processor inside of it.

Each PalmPilot has 256K of non-volatile ROM, where the core operating system and applications are stored, and variable amounts of RAM, where data and other applications are stored. (See Table 1.1 for the specifics of each PalmPilot model's RAM.)

The original Pilot 1000 and 5000 had a low-contrast 2.4 inch by 3.3 inch LCD display. The new PalmPilot Personal and PalmPilot Pro models have the same size display, but add backlight capability and a higher contrast LCD for low-light situations.

The differences between the various Pilot and PalmPilot models are set forth in Table 1.1.

Table 1.1 PalmPilot Model Comparison

Model	Main Apps.	Expense App.	Mail App.	Backlit Memory	HC-LCD
Pilot 1000	✓			128K	No
Pilot 5000	✓			512K	No
PalmPilot Pers.	✓	✓		512K	Yes
PalmPilot Pro.	✓	✓	✓	1M	Yes

Main Applications

All the PalmPilot models come with four main applications that are accessible from the four bottom buttons of the PalmPilot.

Date Book The Date Book has basic time-keeping and reporting capabilities that are similar in design to the agenda page of a paper organizer. But with the PalmPilot, the display can be quickly toggled between Day View and Week View (and Month View with version 2.0). Other features include the option of attaching notes and/or an alarm to each appointment entry.

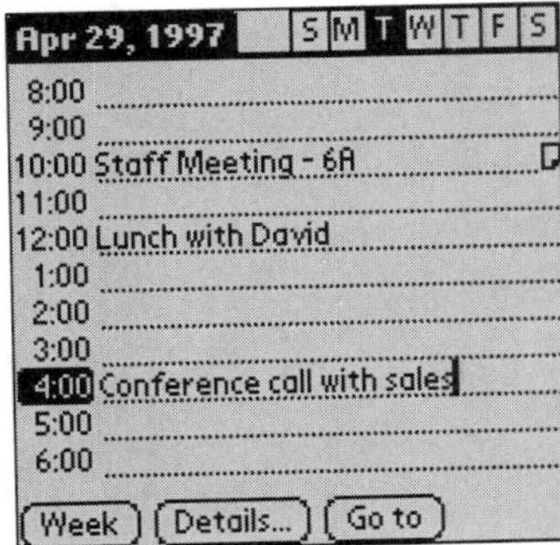

FIGURE 1.2
Date Book items can be added for any time of any day and can have alarms and notes attached.

NOTE Version 2.0 of the PalmPilot operating system adds a Month View to the Date Book application.

Address Book The Address Book will help you attain a new level of organization of names, numbers, addresses, and other pertinent contact information. Each address book entry has the prerequisite name and address fields, as well as five fields for phone numbers or e-mail addresses, and four fields for other pertinent information. As an option, a note can also be attached. Each entry can also include an attached note and can be assigned to user-defined categories for easier grouping and sorting.

FIGURE 1.3
Customize each entry in the Address Book so that it will display the information you need most.

To Do List The To Do List includes categories to sort items that need to be accomplished, by priority, by date due, or in an order defined by the user. As an option, each item can also have a note attached for more details.

Memo Pad Creates free-form notes (up to 4,000 characters) that can be assigned to user-defined categories for grouping and sorting purposes.

FIGURE 1.4
Quickly edit the specifics of your To Do items from the main list.

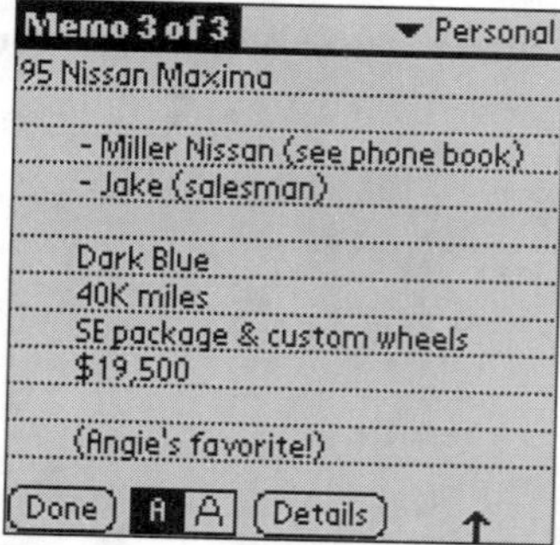

FIGURE 1.5
Keep longer notes in the Memo Pad by using shortcuts to make data entry easier.

Calculator The Calculator is a numeric calculator that handles basic arithmetic functions, memory save and recall, as well as cut and paste from other applications.

NOTE The original version of the PalmPilot Calculator (shipped with the 1000 and 5000) has a few inconsistencies that can lead to unreliable calculations. If you have a 1000 or 5000, check your Calculator and make sure it has the longer "+" key, as shown in Figure 1.6. If it does not, download the SLIMCALC patch from the official PalmPilot Web Site (**www.usr.com/palm**) or call 3Com Corporation to obtain it. ■

FIGURE 1.6
The Calculator is somewhat limited, but its large buttons make it easy to use your fingers for quick calculations.

Security The Security utility allows you to protect your PalmPilot with a password and to hide personal records.

FIGURE 1.7
The Security features consist of a function to hide personal records and a password to unlock the PalmPilot.

PalmPilot Applications

The PalmPilot models add three new applications to the main group of PalmPilot applications: PalmPilot Expense, TCP/IP, and PalmPilot Mail.

PalmPilot Expense, included with both the Personal and Professional PalmPilot, provides the capability to enter expenses by category, HotSync the data to the desktop, and export the expenses to an Excel-compatible spreadsheet. PalmPilot Expense doesn't have many frills, but accomplishes the basic tasks of tracking and reporting expenses.

NOTE See Appendix B, "Software Compendium," for information about third-party expense software with more capabilities.

PalmPilot TCP/IP comes with the PalmPilot Professional and provides basic TCP/IP connectivity through the serial interface. Note that this only provides a TCP/IP connection; additional software is necessary to view data received over the connection.

NOTE See Appendix B, "Software Compendium," for information about third-party TCP/IP software.

PalmPilot Mail uses TCP/IP, Windows MAPI, or VIM protocol to send and receive e-mail. The TCP/IP connectivity can send and receive mail directly from a remote mailbox, while the MAPI/VIM interface can synchronize mail with any MAPI- or VIM-compatible mail client.

NOTE MAPI-compatible mail clients include Microsoft Exchange and Lotus cc:Mail. Check your documentation or ask your system administrator to find out if your mail system is MAPI- or VIM-compliant.

Additional Applications

As previously stated, the main draw to the PalmPilot is the ability to program and add additional applications to the device. Although it was primarily designed as an electronic organizer, the Pilot 1000 quickly became a platform for almost every application imaginable, supplied by many third-party developers.

NOTE The additional software can be found in several locations, ranging from the World Wide Web (start at **www.usr.com/palm/pilot-links.html**), to collections available on CD-ROM (and in the back of this book). See Appendix B, "Software Compendium," for more information about add-on software.

Some of the more popular applications include:

Pocket Chess Provides an intelligent opponent anytime you are in the mood for a good game. Also allows two human opponents to play against one another.

DinkyPad A freehand drawing program that takes advantage of the PalmPilot's touch screen.

DigiClock, **PilotClock**, etc. Large, full-screen digital and analog clocks.

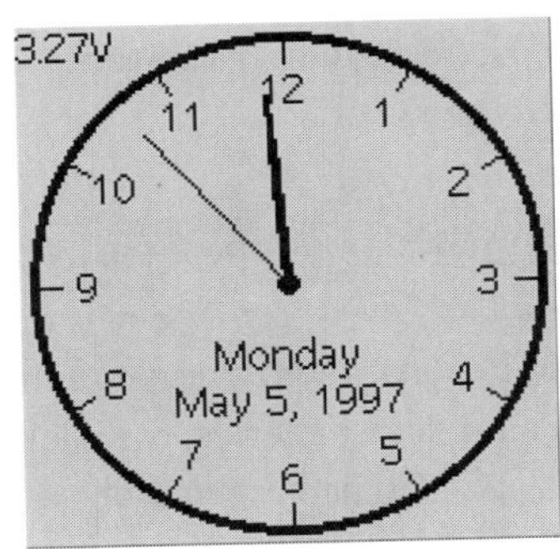

FIGURE 1.8
There is a variety of third-party clocks and timers available for the PalmPilot.

Tricorder A whimsical model of the popular scientific device from *Star Trek*.

Agenda An application that displays the To Do and Agenda items for the current day, week, and month.

MorseCode An application that translates text into variable-speed Morse code.

cbasPad (Chipmunk Basic) A small BASIC programming language for the PalmPilot.

There are also several PC- and Mac-based programs that work with the various PalmPilot applications. These applications include:

Generic Conduit A generic program that allows the transfer of data to and from the PalmPilot.

Icon Editor A Windows application for designing new icons for the Program Launcher screen of the PalmPilot.

CoPilot A PC- and Mac-based PalmPilot emulator for developing and testing PalmPilot applications.

Various Programming Environments Used to develop PalmPilot applications by using everything from BASIC, to C, to Java.

DinkyView and Other PC/Mac-based Viewers Used for viewing PalmPilot data on the PC or Mac.

Backlit Display

The two newest models of the PalmPilot—the PalmPilot Personal and PalmPilot Pro—sport a new backlit display. The new display allows the use of the PalmPilot in total darkness. Although the new display can quickly drain the PalmPilot's batteries, the backlit feature can be turned on and off as needed and it generally isn't needed that often.

PalmPilot Accessories

The PalmPilot has also spawned many add-on products such as specialized styli, cases, and even new wireless modems.

Each PalmPilot model comes with a promotional insert, advertising the variety of accessories available for the PalmPilot. Several of these accessories are available directly from 3Com Corporation, but the majority are manufactured by third-party vendors. (See Appendix A, "PalmPilot Resources," for more information about accessories for your PalmPilot.)

Replacement Stylus Products

There are several replacement stylus products available for the PalmPilot, ranging from the smaller variety that replace the stylus that ships with the PalmPilot, to a stylus refill for several normal pen products.

On the Web, PDA Panache (**www.pdapanache.com**) is leading the pack with several popular stylus products. Their own "Black Nail" replacement stylus fits the stylus slot in the side of the PalmPilot but is weighted to feel more natural when writing. They also carry several pen refills with stylus tips fitting Cross and Mont Blanc pens, a pen/stylus duo product, and a stylus pen with a built-in light for night use.

Most medium- to high-grade pen manufacturers also carry stylus refills for their own pens, turning your favorite pen into your favorite stylus.

Additional Carrying Cases

The slip case that ships with the PalmPilot is ideal for most applications, but several vendors have stepped forward with unique designs for special uses.

Slim Cases Various manufacturers have improved upon the basic PalmPilot case design, adding flip tops and cradle access slots. These replacement cases retain the small size of the standard case, allowing the protected PalmPilot to easily slip into its user's pocket.

Specialty Cases There are also several "deluxe" cases available for the PalmPilot, including a belt pouch and even an insert for your favorite paper organizer product. These cases tend to be slightly larger than the standard case, but allow the user to carry note paper, credit cards, and pen-sized styli along with the PalmPilot itself.

NOTE For the ultimate in protection for your PalmPilot, check out *The Cockpit,* a titanium case from Rhino Skin (**www.rhinoskin.com**).

Additional Hardware

3Com Corporation and other manufacturers have also released numerous hardware products to integrate with the PalmPilot. These products include:

- Additional/replacement HotSync cradles
- Modem and HotSync cables
- Cellular phone (PCSI PAL) adapters
- Leather jackets and T-shirts

With the possible exception of the leather jackets and T-shirts, each of the hardware add-ons were user-inspired. U.S. Robotics showed remarkable insight in listening to the original Pilot 1000 and 5000 owners by providing hardware to help PalmPilot users accomplish their work.

Graffiti

3Com Corporation incorporates the Graffiti handwriting-recognition language for its primary data method. Originally designed for small digital assistants, Graffiti uses a special character set resembling shorthand, uppercase characters.

Using the small data entry pad at the bottom of the display, the user can enter text accurately, up to thirty words-per-minute.

NOTE The "thirty words-per-minute" is marketing hype for Graffiti. Although Graffiti was designed for accurate entry, and proficient users can come close to this limit, the actual entry rate of the casual user will be considerably lower.

Graffiti Basics

Graffiti was developed in 1996 by Palm Computing, Inc. to help the Personal Digital Assistant manufacturers bring handwriting recognition to their platforms. Graffiti succeeded where others had failed by breaking the mold—instead of trying to recognize every user's writing, Graffiti forced the users to learn its way of writing.

The "Graffiti Alphabet" is a series of one-stroke characters, each resembling a capital letter with a few lines missing. For example, the Graffiti "A" is written as a capital "A" without the cross bar.

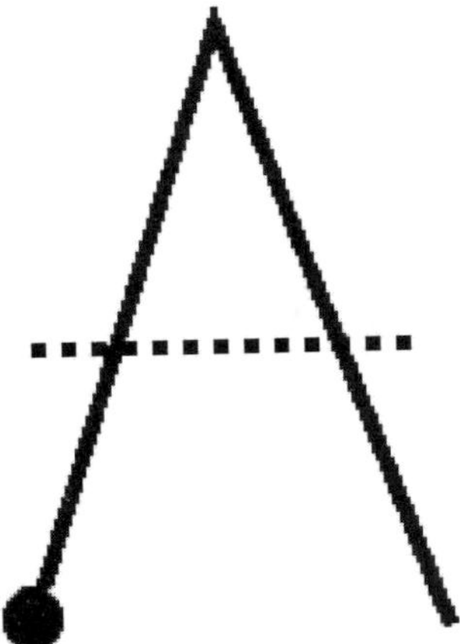

FIGURE 1.9
The Graffiti "A" looks like an upside down "V" at first glance, until you visualizethe missing cross line, shown as a dotted line in the figure.

NOTE Recognizing the likeness to capital letters makes learning Graffiti significantly easier. Instead of trying to learn each Graffiti stroke, try writing capital letters. You will find yourself having to look up only one or two strokes.

The numbers (0-9) are just as intuitive as the letters A-Z, but other characters can be a bit more arcane. For example, the stroke for the pound sign, #, shown in Figure 1.10, doesn't readily jump to mind—so keep that quick reference card handy!

NOTE The Graffiti quick reference card that comes with the PalmPilot lists almost every stroke you can enter into the PalmPilot. Its business card size makes it easy to carry in your PalmPilot's case, or even in your wallet.

Also, don't forget to use the Graffiti reference stickers that come with the PalmPilot. Put the basic reference on the back of your PalmPilot until you are familiar with those strokes, and then replace it with the shift/extended sticker.

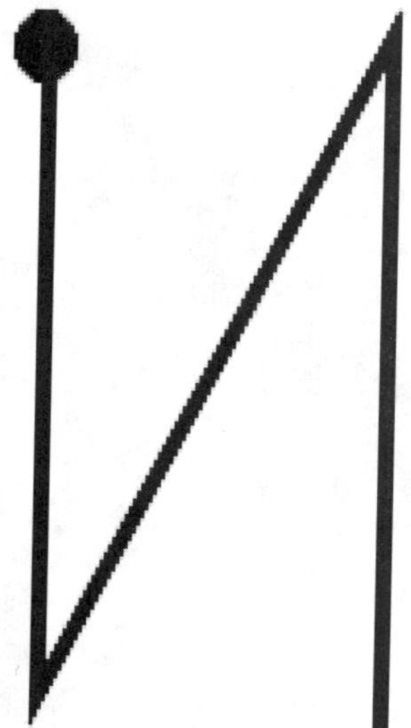

FIGURE 1.10
The Graffiti stroke for the pound sign (#), after a punctuation shift (.).

Graffiti Tips

Learning and using Graffiti isn't hard, but the learning curve can be steep for some users. The following short tips will help you learn and use Graffiti more efficiently:

- Write at normal speed

  Don't try to write slower or faster than you do normally. Writing quickly causes your movements to be less accurate and, therefore, more error prone. Contrary to what you might think, writing slowly can also cause recognition errors (on top of making your text entry painfully slow!).

- Use large strokes

  You will find that you have a tendency to write your strokes quite small in the Graffiti entry area. This is due to the slippery nature of the PalmPilot's glass, the confining boundary of the entry area, and the weight and size of the stylus. The smaller your strokes become, the harder it is for Graffiti to recognize them.

- Use a different stylus

  If you are prone to writing a lot in your PalmPilot, invest in a pen stylus from 3Com Corporation or one of the PDA Pen manufacturers. (See Appendix A, "PalmPilot Resources" for more information on replacement styli.) You will be amazed at the difference a correctly weighted stylus makes.

- Make the Graffiti entry area more friendly

  Most people aren't used to writing on glass with plastic pens. The glass is slippery and the plastic tends to slide around quite a bit. Try putting a small Post-It note over the Graffiti area to simulate the friction of writing on paper. Other users have used Post-It tape, 3M clear tape products, and screen protectors made specifically for the PalmPilot. (See Appendix A, "PalmPilot Resources," for more information on screen-protecting products.)

- Use alternate characters

  There will be one or two characters that consistently cause you problems. For example, you might consistently get "U" when you try to write a "V." If a variant exists for your problem character, use it instead. For the example here, the backward variant of "V" is distinct enough from "U" to never cause a problem.

- One Word: Shortcuts

  There will be at least ten words or phrases that you find yourself writing over and over again. Identify these words or phrases and enter them into your Shortcuts so they can be entered with only a few short strokes. Common words and phrases to look for include your name, your company name, and words like "meeting" or "lunch."

- Learn the editing strokes

  Learning how to move the cursor around and cut, copy, and paste can save you lots of data-entry time. Read through the Graffiti section of the PalmPilot manual and pay particular attention to the "Advanced Strokes" section.

General PalmPilot Use

The PalmPilot makes a cool toy. Almost everyone who sees it says, "I have to get one of those!" However, the PalmPilot makes an even better tool, whether a simple replacement for your paper-based organizer, a mobile e-mail device, or a development platform for applications.

But, just how do you maximize your use of the PalmPilot? Simple: Use it and don't believe there is anything it can't do.

PalmPilot versus Windows CE

Many people have compared or sought to compare the PalmPilot to the new Windows CE devices on the market. These people are missing the point—they are comparing apples to oranges.

The PalmPilot was developed to be a portable, connected, electronic organizer. That means it has a date book, to do list, phone book, and memo pad. The PalmPilot will keep you on time and organized.

Windows CE was developed to be a portable computing solution. This means it has an actual word processor (complete with spell check), spreadsheet, and so on. Windows CE gives you actual portable computing power in a familiar environment.

If you need an organizer, but don't want the overhead of a full operating system and computer power, stick with the PalmPilot. If you want a portable Windows solution, but don't want the size or cost of a notebook computer, opt for a Windows CE device instead.

Start by taking your PalmPilot everywhere you go and use it whenever possible. Track your day in the Date Book, keep your contacts in the Phone Book, add and check off items in the To Do list, and take notes in the Memo Pad. Learn to use alarms, categories, and the Find feature.

If you find yourself wanting the PalmPilot to do more for you, take a trip on the Internet and look for add-on applications that might suit your needs. If you don't find what you need, ask for it on the news groups, forums, or mailing lists. If you are adventurous, grab a development tool and make the right tool yourself.

TIP You might be surprised at how versatile the built-in applications can be. For example, if you need a grocery list, try creating a "Grocery" category in the To Do application. Enter your grocery list under this new category and check off items while you shop.

CHAPTER 2

Staying On Time

The PalmPilot makes an excellent timepiece, having an internal realtime clock. Of course, we aren't talking about buying a wrist strap and wearing it like a Rolex. With its built-in Date Book, add-on applications, and processing power, the PalmPilot is more like a sophisticated alarm clock and personal assistant rolled into one.

This chapter will show you how the PalmPilot can be used to keep your schedule and help ensure you hold to it.

Good PalmPilot Habits

Before delving into how to use the PalmPilot for your agenda, let's take a second or two to talk about good "PalmPilot habits" for staying on time.

Keep It Nearby

In order for the PalmPilot to alert you of activities and appointments, it must be kept nearby. If you leave your PalmPilot on your desk while you are out running errands, it cannot be effective.

Although the PalmPilot's small size provides for easy carrying in shirt and jacket pockets and purses, doing so is not the answer for all users. Some users prefer to carry it like a paper organizer, in its own case, complete with credit cards, pens, extra paper, and so on. Other users prefer the convenience of the belt clip case, keeping the PalmPilot as handy as their pager.

NOTE Devout users of paper organizers should have no problem getting used to having their PalmPilot close at hand. After carrying a few pounds of paper around, the PalmPilot's 5.7 ounces should come as a relief! However, several users have opted for the *Franklin Day Planner* case for the PalmPilot. This case allows the PalmPilot to be carried in the standard Franklin Day Planner binder. ■

With all the options currently available for carrying and protecting your PalmPilot, it is easy to find a solution that fits your needs. Consider the following when exploring your options:

- Do you frequently need access to your PalmPilot, or do you use it only occasionally?
- Will you use your PalmPilot only for business-related tasks, or for personal ones as well?
- What else do you need quick and frequent access to that can be combined with your PalmPilot?
- How active are you during the day? Are you in and out of meetings?
- Do you typically carry a date planner?

Examine your answers to these questions and determine how often you will need to access your PalmPilot, how quick each access needs to be, and the protection you must have for your PalmPilot's safety.

NOTE Users of paper organizers are probably used to carrying fairly large binders, with their organizer secured within. These binders typically enable you to carry multiple pens, scratch paper, as well as business and credit cards. If you are used to having those extra items handy, opt for a larger PalmPilot case that can accommodate them. The goal is to make your PalmPilot perform much like your paper organizer to ease your transition to the PalmPilot. ■

Those users that need quick and frequent access should opt for one of the flip-top cases, like the E&B Pilot Glove II. Those that need more storage for additional items (credit cards, pens, etc.) should opt for cases like the Deluxe Leather Case from 3Com Corporation or the Pilot Ware *Pilot Pouch*.

Once you find a solution for carrying your PalmPilot, carry it with you wherever you go. Shortly, you will find where you need it and where you don't, but you will never be at a loss.

TIP Your PalmPilot will come in handy in more instances than you might think. The Memo Pad enables you to take quick notes, whether in an important meeting or shopping for a new car. The Address Book enables you to enter that elusive telephone number after dialing information for the up-teenth time, and the To Do list helps you remember to pick up milk on your way home.

Date Book Options

Optimizing the display of the Date Book can help you stay organized and on top of your daily agenda. The PalmPilot offers several options that can be tuned to suit your individual needs.

NOTE Find the Date Book Preferences under Menu, Option, Preferences while the Date Book is running.

Start and End Times If your typical day starts at 8A.M., it does little good to display times starting at 7A.M., or 9A.M. This is also applicable to the time you usually end your day.

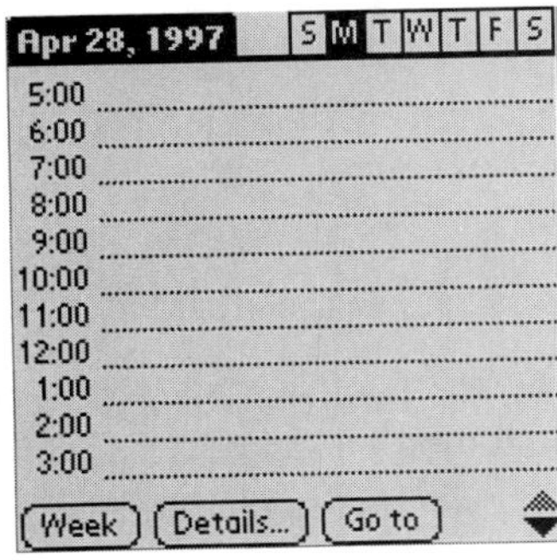

FIGURE 2.1
Too wide of a time range doesn't allow you to see much of the day.

If you choose to display times outside of your normal workday, you will have less room to display the times that encompass your workday. Conversely, if you don't display your entire workday, entering

STAYING ON TIME

appointments at the beginning or end of the day becomes more difficult—you have to use the New button and manually enter the time instead of just clicking the appropriate time in the Day View.

NOTE You can use the New button to add appointments for any time of the day, despite the times automatically displayed by the Preferences setting.

Display Options Users of OS 2.x have several more display options from which to choose for their Day and Month Views.

In Day View, you can show time bars, which visually depict the length of time an appointment or event encompasses. You can also compress the Day View to conserve space on-screen. Compressing the Day View removes empty time slots from the bottom of the screen.

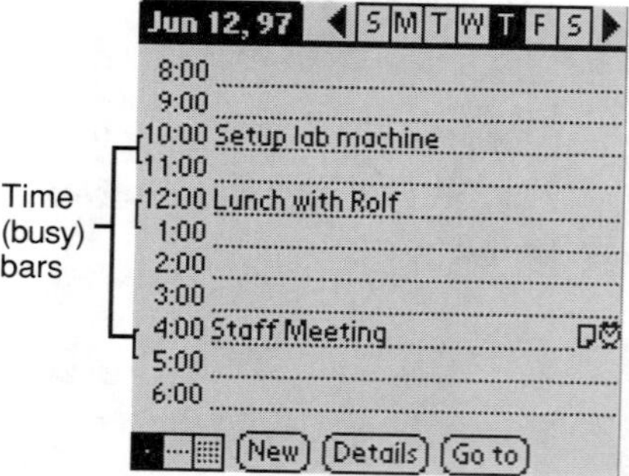

FIGURE 2.2
Time bars help you see the actual length of your appointments.

The Display Options for Month View control what type of events are displayed in the view—timed, untimed, reoccurring, or any combination of the three. Each type of event is depicted by a different mark on the appropriate day.

Knowing the Time

One drawback to the 3Com Corporation PalmPilot is its lack of a current time display. Although an appointment can be set with an alarm to warn you of an upcoming event, it is always useful to know the current time.

Users of the 1.x operating system (OS) can only view the time in two places:

- The Preferences screen
- The bottom of the Application Launcher

PalmPilot users that have OS 2.x have one extra place to view the time: by clicking the Date Tab on top of the Day View of the Date Book.

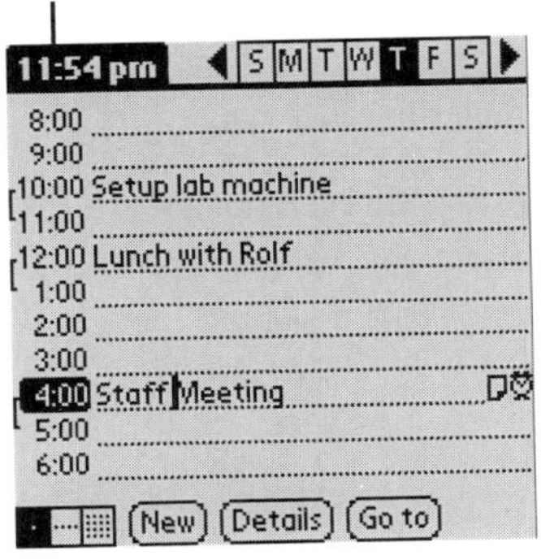

FIGURE 2.3
The current time is readily accessible in the Date Book (OS 2.x only).

Because of this shortcoming, the first few third-party applications developed for the Pilot 1000 and 5000 were clocks. There are several clocks of differing types available, from the simple digital variety, to clocks that show the time around the world.

TIP Use SilkHack or the PalmPilot's OS 2.x capabilities to redefine a silk- screen button to show your favorite clock. (See Appendix B, "Software Compendium," for more information on SilkHack.)

Basic Timepieces

There are several basic clock programs available for the PalmPilot. This section highlights the more popular applications.

DigiClock DigiClock from StingerSoft is a simple, no-frills digital clock. It shows the current time and date, and that's all.

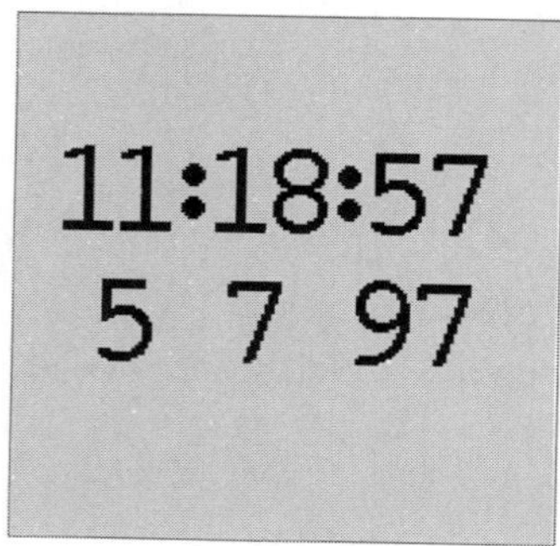

FIGURE 2.4
DigiClock provides a basic digital clock, with large numbers for easy viewing.

Analog Clock Mike Carlton's Analog Clock displays the current time on a simple clock dial, with optional day/date and battery meter display. Analog Clock can also display the second hand and can be configured to audibly "tick."

FIGURE 2.5
The Analog Clock provides a more traditional timepiece.

pilotClock If you are looking for a bit more functionality in the clock for your PalmPilot, check out pilotClock by Little Wing Software. pilotClock displays the current date and time, and optionally, battery voltage and the time in a time zone you choose.

Besides offering a clock, pilotClock also has a stopwatch, nine configurable alarms, and a timer.

FIGURE 2.6
pilotClock is a full-featured timepiece, with time, date, and stopwatch capabilities.

You can use pilotClock for a variety of tasks, from simply finding out the current time, to setting a timer to check on dinner.

Outside Your Time Zone

Businesspersons and frequent travelers often need to keep track of several different time zones. The basic PalmPilot OS doesn't have any provisions for keeping track of other time zones, but there are several add-on programs that provide this function.

World Time World Time, by Creative Digital Publishing, enables you to view the current time of more than 260 countries, cities, and time zones around the world. You simply select your current time zone, and World Time synchronizes the rest of the time zones according to the current time.

World Time enables you to designate entries as "special." These entries can then be viewed separately in their own list. This feature is perfect for keeping track of a few key locations—avoiding the accidental 3A.M. phone call to the key account in Turkey! You can also look up locations by entering the first few characters of the location on the Graffiti pad.

World Time		▼ All
Australia, NSW	11:34 pm	5/7/97
Albania	* 3:34 pm	5/7/97
Aleutian Isles	* 4:34 am	5/7/97
Algeria	2:34 pm	5/7/97
Anchorage	* 5:34 am	5/7/97
Angola	2:34 pm	5/7/97
Argentina	10:34 am	5/7/97
Arizona	6:34 am	5/7/97
Armenia	* 5:34 pm	5/7/97
Aruba	9:34 am	5/7/97
Athens	* 4:34 pm	5/7/97
Atlanta	* 9:34 am	5/7/97
Auckland	1:34 am	5/8/97

FIGURE 2.7
World Time shows the current time for over 260 locations worldwide.

Although World Time performs its task admirably, it is perhaps better suited for the executive who deals with clients in different time zones than for the frequent traveler.

Abroad! Abroad!, by Yoshimitsu Kanai, can be an international traveler's best friend. Besides keeping track of the time in several configurable cities, Abroad! also calculates currency exchanges and converts common units between English and metric values.

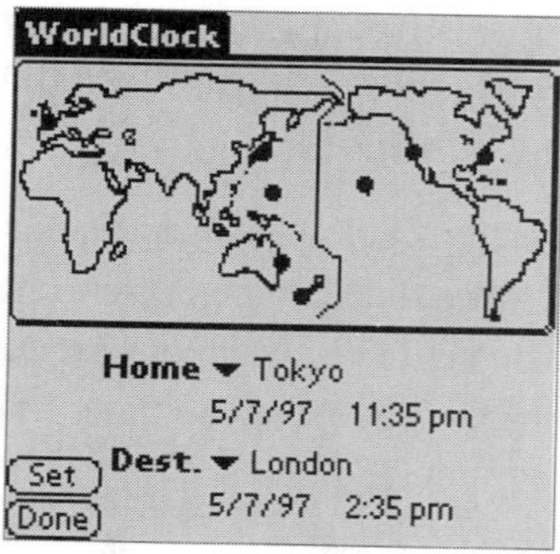

FIGURE 2.8
Abroad! lets you define multiple cities for easy access when traveling between them.

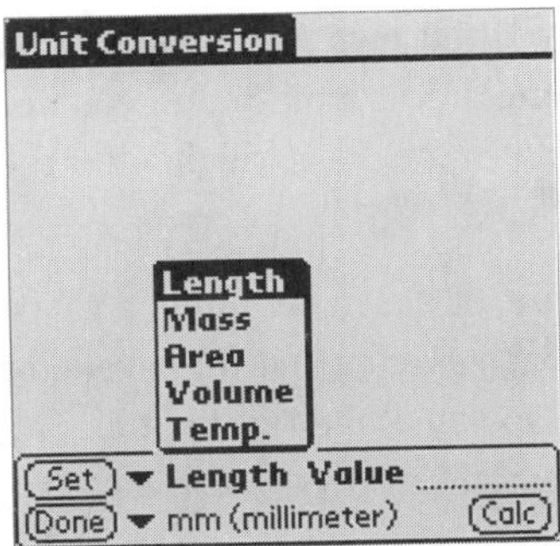

FIGURE 2.9
Abroad's multiple conversion features enable you to easily convert units from different systems.

Although Abroad! offers a lot to the traveler, it has too much overhead if you only need a simple clock.

Using Basic Alarms

The PalmPilot's Date Book includes basic alarms that can be set for each event entered. Each alarm can be set to ring any number of minutes, hours, or days ahead of the event to which it is attached.

When the specified time arrives, the PalmPilot will sound its default alarm chirp and display the text describing the event to which it is attached. You acknowledge the alarm by touching the OK button on the alarm screen. Unanswered alarms will remain on the screen and subsequent alarms will stack up on top of it.

NOTE If you do not acknowledge an alarm and are using OS 2.x or above, the PalmPilot will continue to sound the alarm every few minutes through the duration of the appointment.

Managing Repeating Events

Repeating events, like regularly scheduled meetings, are prime candidates for "right-before-the-event" alarms. Such alarms simply remind you of the current time.

However, repeating events have their own management challenges. When you move or change a one-time appointment, you don't have to worry about what the reoccurring events will do after the moved event.

When you change the date, time, or alarm setting of a reoccurring event, you are given the chance to change just that event, or all the reoccurring events. Be careful to select the right option or risk changing more than you bargained for!

NOTE Be aware that changing or deleting "ALL" reoccurrences under Pilot OS 1.x will also change or delete any *previous* events. PalmPilots using OS 2.x will only change reoccurrences after the selected event.

Managing Appointments and Events

Everyone's schedule changes, frequently without notice. Thankfully, managing your appointments with the PalmPilot is relatively easy.

Quick Changes

You can quickly change aspects of any appointment by touching the pertinent field on the Date Book screen. For example, to change the time for a particular appointment, simply touch the date of the appointment and the Set Time dialog box dutifully appears.

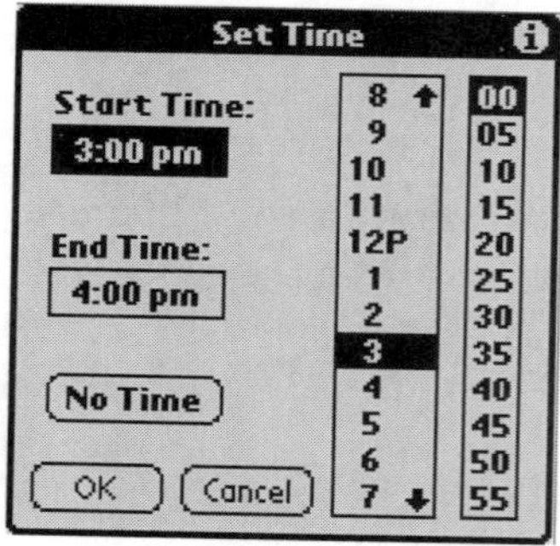

FIGURE 2.10

Touch the corresponding time in the day view to get the Set Time dialog box for that event.

If an appointment has a note attached, a note icon will appear in the right margin. You can touch this note to open it, and then read or edit it appropriately.

TIP Use the Notes feature to contain the agenda of a particular meeting, or directions to the location of an appointment. The Notes feature keeps important information close to the events that require it.

On the OS 2.x models, icons representing the alarm are also displayed along the right margin. Touching the small alarm clock will cause the Event Details dialog box to appear.

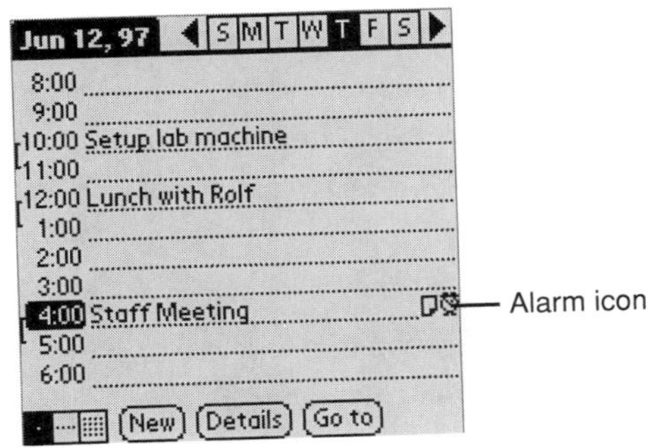

FIGURE 2.11
Touch the alarm clock to change the event's alarm setting

The Week and Month Views

You also can view your appointments and events by the week and, if you have OS 2.x, by the month. The Week View shows shaded blocks where you have appointments. This view can be used to quickly assess your free time.

TIP Users of OS 2.x can view the text of their appointments in the Week View by tapping each appointment. Appointments can be moved around the current week by tapping and dragging them to a new time slot. Be sure to check neighboring appointments when you drop the appointment in its new spot, lest you schedule an out-of-town meeting right after an in-house one!

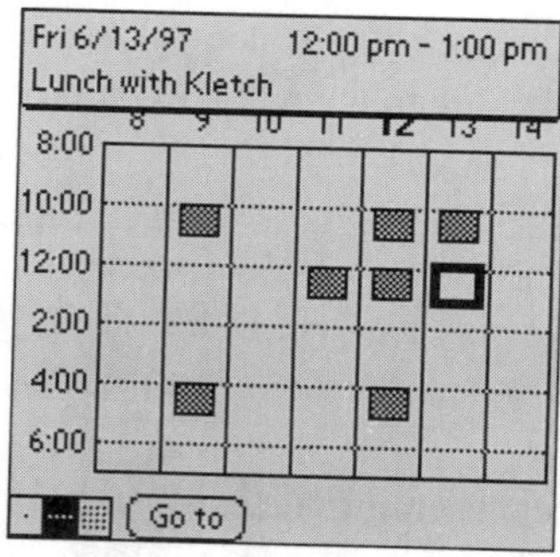

FIGURE 2.12
Drag and drop appointments with OS 2.x.

The month view (OS 2.x only) is of limited value. This view only shows on which days you have appointments; you cannot view or change appointments in this view. However, touching a date will take you to that date's day view, where you can edit the appointments.

Agenda

Agenda by DovCom is an application that shows you your appointments for today, tomorrow, or the current week. Agenda also displays any outstanding To Do items. The icons at the bottom of Agenda can also reset, turn off, and turn lock your PalmPilot.

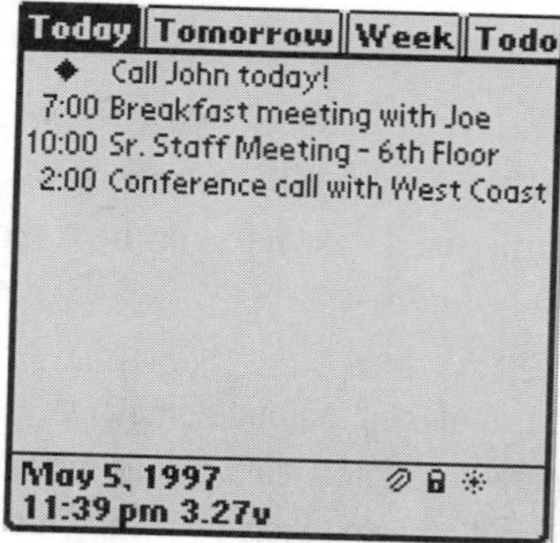

FIGURE 2.13
Get a quick list of your Agenda.

Agenda is a must for the busy professional who needs to stay abreast of his or her future commitments. It makes a great compliment to the OS 2.x views, enabling you to see your appointments and events in a concise view before you set off to edit them.

Advanced Alarms and Reminders

Although the PalmPilot's basic alarm functions work well for timed events, there is little provision for *reminders*—alarms that signal a special day or untimed event. There are several solutions for reminders, each of which is covered in a section below.

Using Untimed Events

It is possible to use the built-in Date Book for general reminders, as well as alarms for events. To set a general reminder, create an event and set the time to No Time. This creates what is known as an untimed event, to which you can attach an alarm.

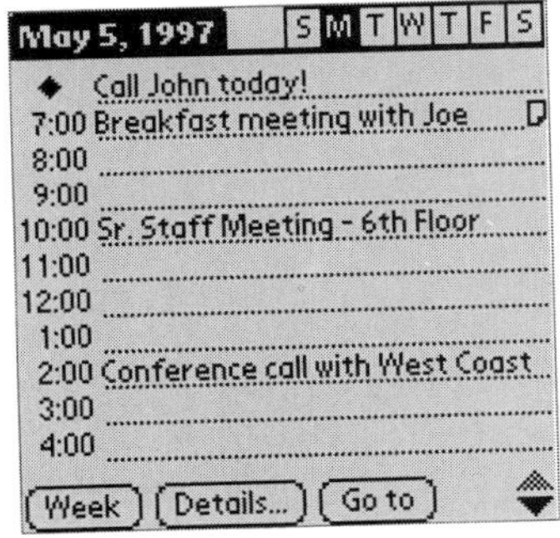

FIGURE 2.14
Untimed events appear at the top of the Day View.

Even though an event is set with "No Time," it actually does have a time, namely 12:00A.M. Any attached alarms will be triggered at the appropriate time before 12:00A.M. on that day. For example, a "5 minute" alarm on an untimed event will activate at 11:55P.M. on the previous day.

You can use reminders to keep track of birthdays, bill payment days, and so on. By setting reminder events as untimed, they do not clutter your normal agenda. Because the alarms are based around 12A.M., they are generally the first thing you see the first time you use your PalmPilot that day.

Add-On Reminder Programs

There are several add-on programs that can create better reminders than using untimed events.

Birthdate One of the most popular add-on programs for the PalmPilot is Birthdate, by Fahl Software. This program functions as a birthday reminder, keying off Address Book entries.

To use Birthdate, simply rename one of the Custom fields in the Address Book to Birthdate and enter a person's birthday in this new field. Birthdate then reads these fields and automatically reminds you (via untimed events in the Date Book) of those dates. Birthdate also calculates the person's age, which optionally can be displayed in the reminder.

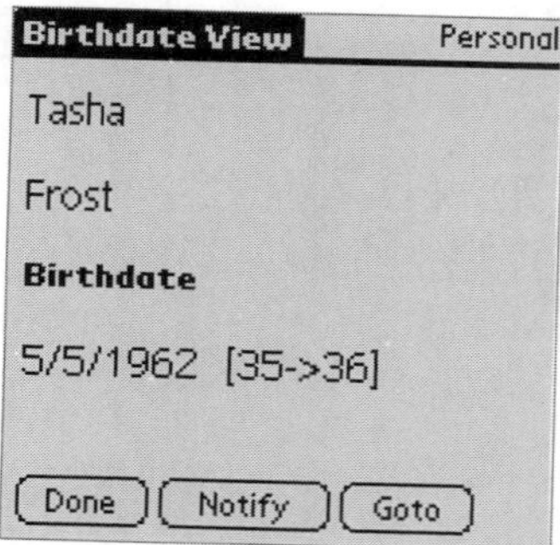

FIGURE 2.15
Birthdate reminds you to send cards, flowers, or a sympathy card.

NOTE The evaluation copy of Birthdate allows you to set up to nine reminders and does not support automatic Date Book entries—you have to select each record and choose "Notify in Date Book" from the program's menu.

LookAtMe LookAtMe, by Bill Ezell, is the ultimate application for reoccurring reminders. This program enables you to set alarms for anytime/day during the week and, optionally, to have an application pop-up after the alarm.

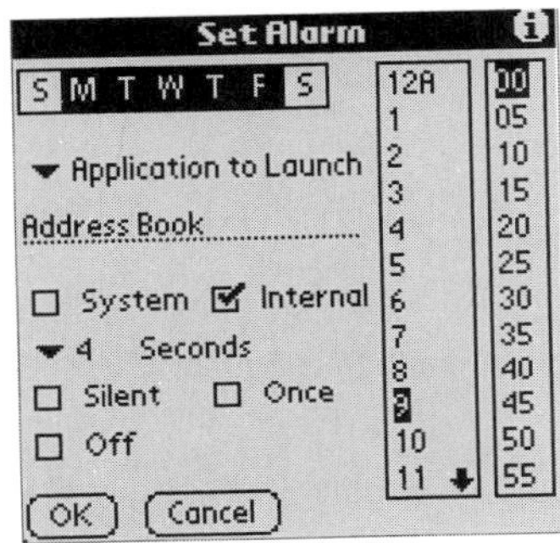

FIGURE 2.16
Set the time, date, and application to launch.

You can use LookAtMe to display your To Do List every day at 9A.M., or bring up your Memo Pad just in time for the staff meeting on Tuesdays at 2P.M.

Accounting for Your Time

If you need to account for your time, the Expense application that comes with the new PalmPilot Pro can help. However, it is only of limited value for tracking billable time. It is designed to track expenses incurred—like dinner with a client. However, some third-party applications have been developed for time accounting by using the PalmPilot. Several of these solutions are examined in the sections that follow.

PalmPilot Expense

The new OS 2.x includes an Expense application, which is designed to keep track of business (and personal) expenses. However, you can use it for limited time tracking as well.

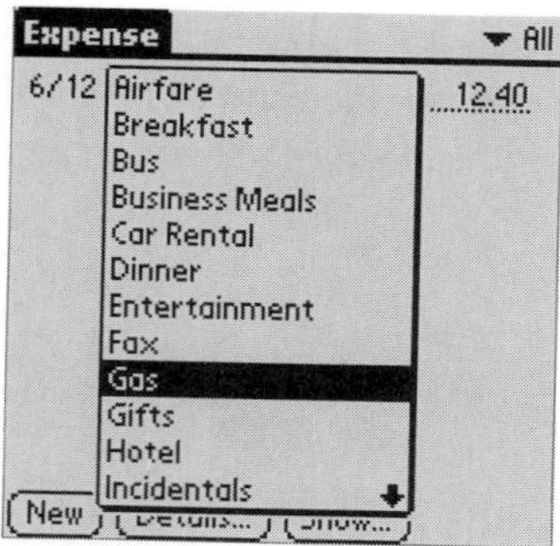

FIGURE 2.17
The OS 2.x Expense application enables you to track expenses and limited expensed time.

The only catch to using the Expense application is that it can't track actual time, only the monetary amount you bill for it. For example, if you charge $50 for an hour of your time and spend an hour and a half on the phone with a client, you cannot enter "1.5 hours" into the Expense application. Instead, you must enter the "$75" total and use a category like "Other" or "Telephone."

NOTE The reporting capability of the Expense application can be used to provide more support for non-dollar-amount expenses. Once your expense have been HotSynced to the desktop and exported to an Excel spreadsheet, you can use the power of Excel to calculate additional values. For example, try entering your time (in hours/minutes) and calculating the dollar amount in Excel.

TimeReporter

TimeReporter, by iambic Software, is an application designed specifically for tracking time. TimeReporter keeps track of your clients/projects/activities (name, id/code, and rate charged), supports time being entered directly or via an integrated stopwatch, enables events to be categorized, and gives you daily totals.

FIGURE 2.18
Add a client, project, or activity...

FIGURE 2.19
...and let TimeReporter keep track of the billing.

A special synchronization application enables you to transfer your time files to your PC in delimited format, ready for import into your favorite spreadsheet or other application.

Hourz

Hourz, by ZöskWare, is another time-recording and reporting application for the PalmPilot. Hourz allows you to enter dates, times, and rates into categorized records and then export them (as a delimited file) to the desktop.

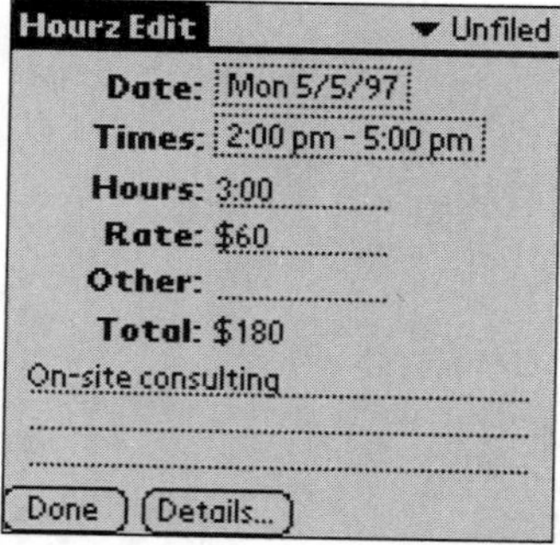

FIGURE 2.20
Keep track of your billable time using Hourz's easy-entry format.

CHAPTER 3

Staying Organized

Managing a busy life is a full-time job. All the details of a business and a personal life must be kept in sync or chaos surely ensues. Whether you work nine-to-five or put in sixty hours a week, whether you are a self-proclaimed "couch potato" or are involved in many extra-curricular activities, the PalmPilot can help you keep all the details organized. This chapter will highlight several techniques and utilities to help you stay organized, whatever your schedule might be.

Organizing Your PalmPilot

Of course, before you can use your PalmPilot to stay organized, your PalmPilot has to be organized. Let's look at several ways to manage the information on your PalmPilot.

Organizing Your Applications

This chapter, like the other chapters in this book, will introduce several new PalmPilot utilities and applications. Although you probably won't be using all of them, your Application Launcher will still fill up as you add some of these utilities and applications to your collection.

FIGURE 3.1
The Application Launcher screen displays installed applications alphabetically, twelve items at a time.

The Application Launcher will hold as many application icons as your memory can hold applications, but using it to find and launch frequently used applications can be a pain. However, there are various methods available to organize the Application Launcher and to define the silkscreen and main application buttons on the PalmPilot. This section will cover the most popular applications.

Deleting Unused Applications The easiest way to help organize the Application Launcher is by installing only the applications you use often, and deleting the applications you seldom use.

To delete an application, choose the Memory application from the Application Launcher and touch the Delete Apps button on the bottom of the Memory screen. Select the application from the list displayed and then touch the Delete button. After confirming your choice, the application and any of its data files will be deleted from memory.

CAUTION Always back up your PalmPilot before deleting any applications you have used. This will help protect against inadvertently losing irreplaceable data.

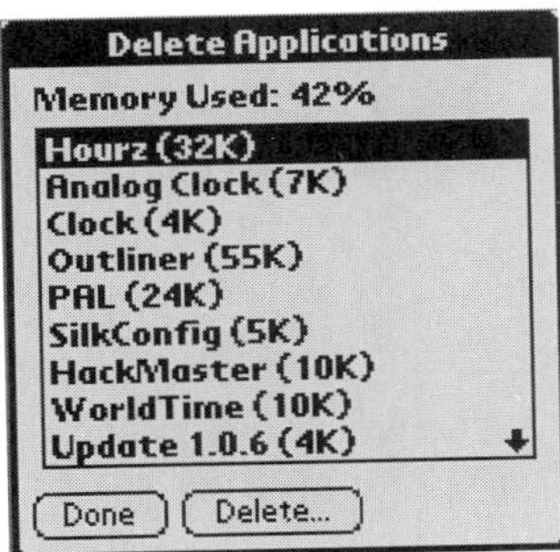

FIGURE 3.2
The Memory application displays the installed applications and their associated memory use.

TIP If you are using OS 1.0.4 or lower, upgrade immediately to OS 1.0.6 or higher. Earlier operating systems were prone to memory fragmentation when applications and data were installed and then deleted. This results in inefficient use of system RAM and the possible inability to install additional applications, even if the total free RAM would allow it. Operating systems 1.0.6 and greater reallocate RAM as needed, keeping fragmentation to a minimum.

If you seem to be having memory allocation problems, you might also want to check out *RipCord* from Harry Ohlsen. RipCord enables you to back up and restore your PalmPilot's RAM and attempts to optimize RAM in the process. (See Appendix B, "Software Compendium" for more information on RipCord.)

SilkHack SilkHack is a hack file from Stingersoft that is designed to work with Edward Keyes' *HackMaster* program. HackMaster is a small application that allows specially written "hack" applications to change the way the basic PalmPilot OS works. For example, SilkHack enables you to change which applications run when you tap the silkscreen buttons on your PalmPilot.

TIP Always back up your PalmPilot before adding and running new hacks for HackMaster. If the hack malfunctions, you may experience data loss.

To use SilkHack, you need to install HackMaster and the two SilkHack files on your PalmPilot. HackMaster takes care of managing the actual hack (SilkHack.prc) file, while the configuration program (SilkConfig.prc) allows you to define what the buttons do.

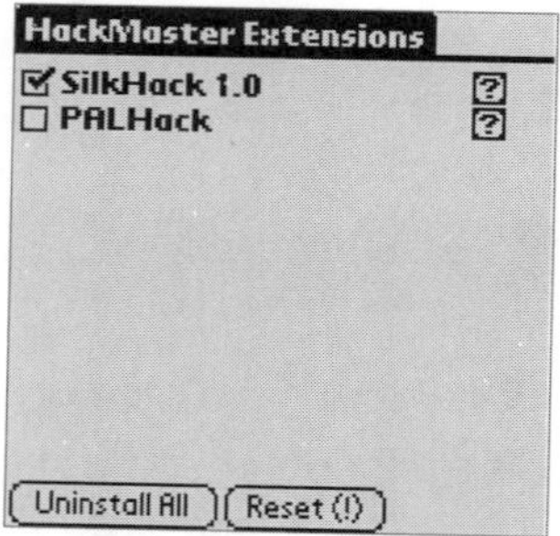

FIGURE 3.3
HackMaster allows you to activate or deactivate any installed hack.

SilkHack divides the four silkscreened buttons into four "quadrants." Each quadrant can be assigned to a different application. To assign an application to a specific quadrant, tap the desired quadrant and then select an application from the list at the left. To return a quadrant to its default setting, tap [Default] on the application list.

NOTE When using SilkConfig, you must first deactivate the SilkHack in HackMaster. After defining your quadrants, you can reactivate the hack. In some cases, you may need to use HackMaster's Reset feature before your new quadrant settings will take effect.

Note that you cannot redefine the upper-left quadrant on the Applications, Menu, and Find buttons. These quadrants can always be used to get to the default applications.

TIP If you are using OS 2.x, setting a Calculator quadrant to Default will launch the application defined in Preferences. (See the following section, "Redefining Buttons in OS 2.x," for more information.)

Redefining Buttons in OS 2.x Users of PalmPilot OS 2.x have a built-in method to change the functionality of the main application buttons. By selecting the Preference application and choosing Buttons from the pull-down menu, you can choose any installed application to be activated from the main application buttons.

NOTE The only silkscreen button you can redefine using this OS 2.x feature is the Calculator button. You must use SilkHack or another utility to redefine the other buttons.

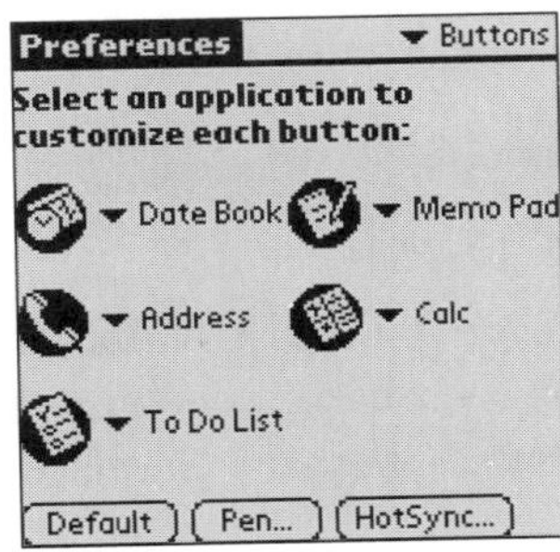

FIGURE 3.4
Use the Buttons Preferences screen to define which applications are activated by the main PalmPilot buttons.

Pilot Application Launcher The Pilot Application Launcher (PAL) is a replacement Application Launcher. When used with HackMaster, PAL directly replaces the built-in Application Launcher with a new interface that enables you to organize your applications into categories. For example, you can organize all of your games into a Games category. Then, when you launch PAL, you can select the Games category to show only your games.

NOTE PAL requires that you have HackMaster installed. After installing the PAL hack, you must enable the hack from the HackMaster main screen.

Like most hacks, PAL requires that you install two files: PALHack.prc (the actual hack) and PAL.prc (the configuration utility for PAL). The interface for PAL is straightforward and resembles the original Application Launcher. The main difference is the small category-selection list at the bottom of the application list, and the reset, lock, and power off icons.

FIGURE 3.5
The PAL screen looks familiar—with a few additions.

To sort your applications into categories, select Edit Apps from the PAL menu. Select each application and a corresponding category. You can add and delete categories using the same interface as other PalmPilot applications.

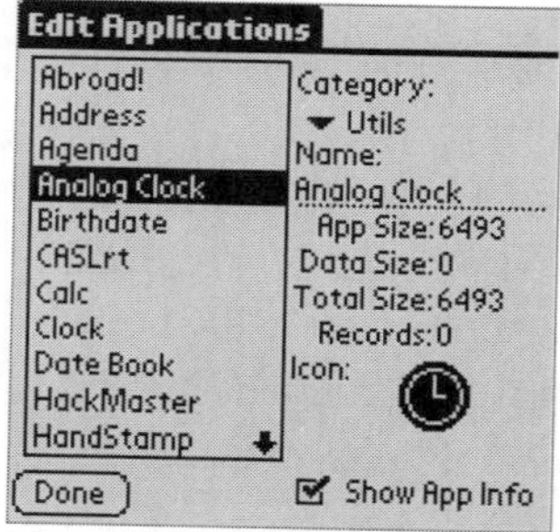

FIGURE 3.6
Placing applications in categories is easy using the PAL interface.

NOTE PAL doesn't keep track of added applications. After adding a new application, you need to use the Update Apps choice from the PAL Menu.

Launch Pad Launch Pad, by Eric Kenslow, is another Application Launcher replacement that is perhaps the most popular. Instead of having a pull-down list to select the category of applications to list, Launch Pad displays individual pages of applications and uses tabs to switch between the pages.

FIGURE 3.7
Launch Pad uses tabbed pages and a graphical interface—simply drag an application to the page on which you want it stored.

You can create as many tabs for application categories as you need. Moving applications between tabs is easy—just tap and hold the application and drag it to the new tab.

Launch Pad has a multitude of options that control how it looks and operates, including whether it takes the place of the built-in PalmPilot Application Launcher. Launch Pad includes icons to show the available memory, to turn off the PalmPilot, and to turn off and lock the PalmPilot. There is even a special pull-down menu containing the common PalmPilot-configuration applications for easy access.

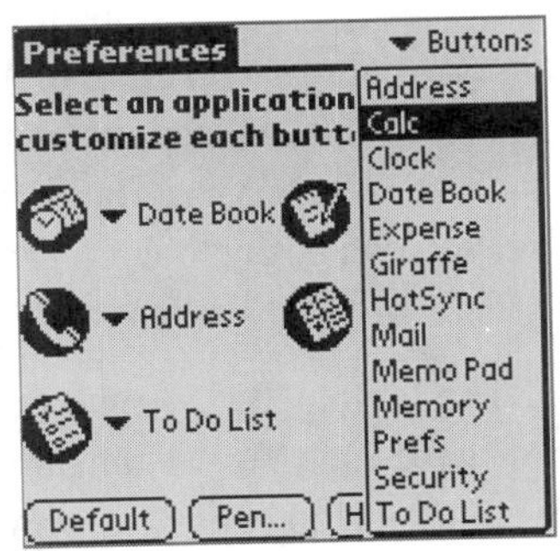

FIGURE 3.8
A multitude of options control Launch Pad's display and operation.

Using Categories

All built-in PalmPilot applications enable you to place records into user-defined categories. Categories enable you to quickly view related records together. For example, the Address Book contains the preset category QuickList for grouping frequently used numbers such as your friends, your doctor, and your lawyer.

Each PalmPilot application (and some third-party applications) can have up to fifteen separate categories defined—each up to fifteen characters long. New records that are created in applications are assigned to the Unfiled category until the record is manually assigned to another category.

NOTE There are actually sixteen possible categories per application, if you count the Unfiled category. However, the Unfiled category cannot be changed or deleted.

If you change the name of a category, that new name will be applied to all records assigned to that category. If you delete a category, all records assigned to that category will be reassigned to the Unfiled category.

Using categories to group related records will help keep your data organized. However, there are other advantages to using categories, as explained in the following sections.

Keeping Track of Projects You can easily keep track of all pieces of a project by defining the same category in every application and assigning all related records to that category. For example, if you are working on a presentation for the national sales meeting in Atlanta, create an "Atlanta Pres" category in all your applications and assign all records for the presentation to the new category. Then, no matter what application you are using, you can easily look up records by referencing that category.

Extra Priority Levels for To Do Items The built-in To Do application enables you to set a numeric priority for each To Do item, and even assign a due date. Using this information, you can sort through your To Do items. However, you can create another organizational and sorting layer to your To Do List by using categories.

For example, create a "Today" category and place within it the items you need to accomplish by the end of the day. At any time, you can select the Today category and instantly see what you still need to accomplish. This method is a little easier than setting the Due Date to "today" and sorting through your whole list.

FIGURE 3.9
Your list of contacts for the Atlanta Presentation are filed under the "Atlanta Pres" category.

NOTE Version 2.x of the PalmPilot OS adds several new features for displaying and sorting To Do items. For example, you can sort your To Do items by category and opt to show as much information as necessary in the main To Do List.

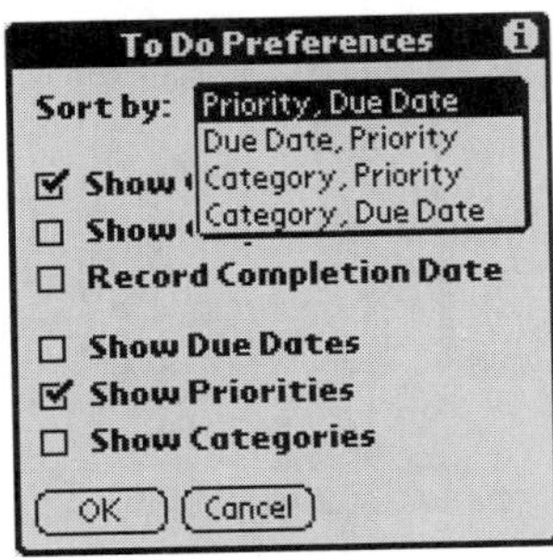

FIGURE 3.10
New sorting and display options help organize To Do items in PalmPilot OS 2.x.

Archiving Old Data Occasionally, you will find several of your databases filling up with old data. You might want to keep this data but not want it to continue to clutter up your workspace. Simply create an "Archive" category and move that data to it. Then you won't see those old records included with your normal data, but you will still have access to them.

TIP You may want to create an Archive category that begins with a subsequent letter of the alphabet, such as *V* or *Z*. When you use an application that can sort records by category, those archived records will appear near the end of the list.

NOTE If space is tight on your PalmPilot, consider using the Archive feature to free up some memory. Just delete the memos you want to archive, making sure that "Save backup copy on PC" is checked before confirming the deletion.

Making the Most of Memo Subjects

You may not realize at first that the first line of your memos in the Memo Pad is the subject that is shown in the main Memo list. Because of this, it is important that you make this first line descriptive of the contents of the memo.

For example, if you commonly take notes in a weekly staff meeting, start each of those memos with "Staff Meeting" and the date. It will then be easy to identify each of your meeting notes in the main memo listing.

TIP Shortcuts are a great way to enter common titles at the top of memos. For example, defining a "sm" shortcut for Staff Meeting can significantly decrease the time it takes to enter the header for the weekly staff meeting.

You can use "@DS" and "@DST" at the *beginning* of a shortcut's text to insert the current date stamp and date/time stamp. Note that these two stamps can be used *only* at the very beginning of shortcut text; they are unrecognized by the system if placed anywhere else.

Losing and Finding Records

No matter how organized you are, sooner or later you will lose some data in your PalmPilot. You have no doubt that the information still exists, yet you have no idea where you put it. That's when Find becomes your best friend.

By tapping the Find button, you activate the Find application of the PalmPilot. This application can quickly sort through all the records on your PalmPilot to locate the information you seek. For example, suppose you meet a new contact during a meeting and add his contact information to a memo you were writing at the time. Several weeks later, you decide to contact him, but can't find the correct memo. Recalling his name was Robert, you fire up Find and search for "Robert." Within seconds, you locate the memo and are on the phone.

FIGURE 3.11
Finding the lost "Robert" information is a cinch.

NOTE In PalmPilot OS 2.x, you can use the Phone Lookup feature of Find to insert information stored in the Address Book into any other application. Simply choose Options, Phone Lookup from the destination application's menu, select the appropriate record from the Address Book display, and select Add. The name and phone number will be added to the current position in the application.

To quickly find and add a record, enter the first few letters of the record you want to add (enough to identify a unique record) and then enter the Phone Lookup command keystroke (/L). The first record that matches the text you entered will be selected.

TIP There are several special shortcuts you can enter into the Find dialog box that affect your PalmPilot's operation. These shortcuts include:

Shortcut	Description
1	A debug mode for programming. This code leaves the serial port open, which can drain your batteries quickly. Perform a soft reset to verify that it is closed.
2	Opens the serial port, which can drain your batteries quickly. Perform a soft reset to verify that it is closed.
3	Sets PalmPilot for "No Auto-Off." Set the appropriate time in Preferences to turn the Auto-off feature back on.
4	Flashes the user name at the bottom of the screen.
5	Removes the user configuration and the HotSync log from the PalmPilot. Perform a hard reset (clearing the PalmPilot) and set the HotSync options to overwrite your PalmPilot data, or risk duplicate entries the next time you HotSync.
6	Displays the ROM date.
7	Toggles the battery monitor between NiCad and Alkaline mode. Using the wrong setting will cause the battery meter to display improperly.

To use these shortcuts, open the Find window and then enter the shortcut Graffiti stroke, a period, and the number of the functions you want. Tap the OK button to activate the function.

CAUTION Some of these special shortcuts can be destructive. Use them carefully, and *at your own risk*.

Using Outlining

The best way to organize a task is to outline the steps it requires. Although this can be done, to some extent, in the Memo Pad or To Do list, Florent Pillet's *Outliner* performs this task much better.

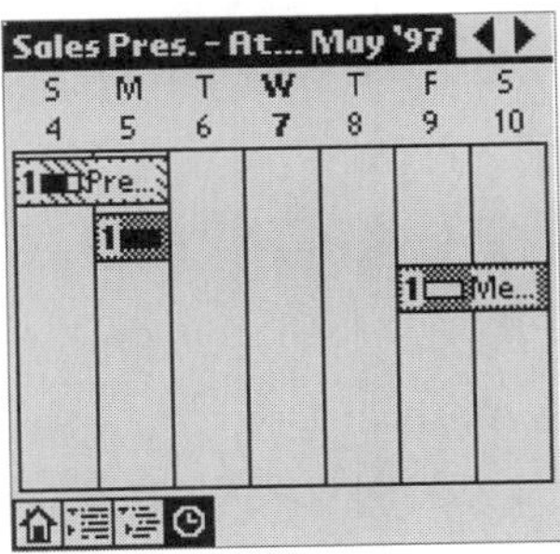

FIGURE 3.12
The Planning view of Outliner shows a Gantt chart of all the items in the outline.

Items in each outline can be promoted or demoted, expanded or collapsed, and moved at will. Each item's sub-items will follow the movement of the main item. Outliner supports numbered (legal) or lettered outline styles and the information displayed in the outline can be customized to fit your needs.

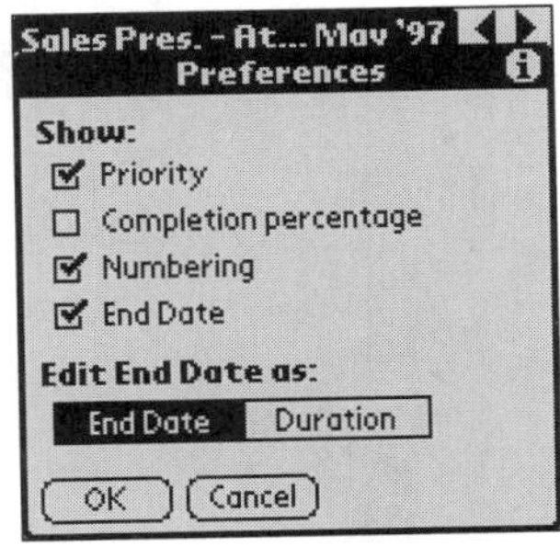

FIGURE 3.13
Select the information that you need Outliner to display.

Outliner can even export your outlines to Memo Pad as text, tab delimited files, or HTML files. You can then HotSync the new memo to your desktop.

CHAPTER 4

Staying Informed

You can use the PalmPilot's Memo Pad to take on-the-spot notes, whether you're jotting down a grocery list, writing down directions to a friend's lake cottage, or taking minutes during an important meeting, the PalmPilot keeps track of it all. This chapter highlights effective use of the PalmPilot's built-in Memo Pad, as well as some third-party text and documentation applications.

Using the Memo Pad

The PalmPilot's Memo Pad is a basic, text-only editor that is designed to hold small memos, each up to 4,000 characters. Like other databases, you can assign the memos in the Memo Pad database to user-defined categories for easier sorting.

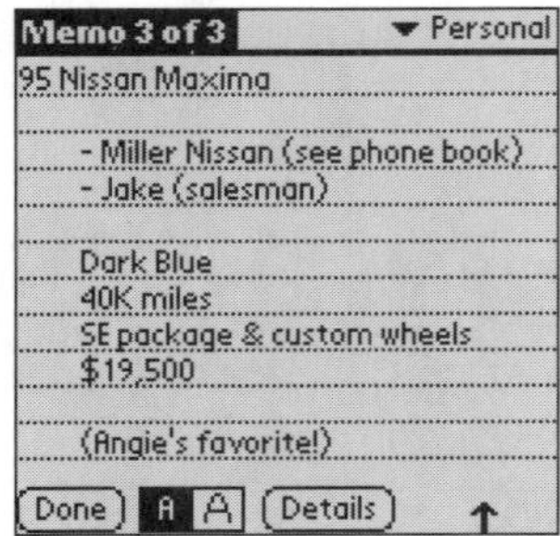

FIGURE 4.1
Memo Pad enables you to enter up to 4,000 characters of plain-text notes.

The type and amount of information you can store in Memo Pad is only limited by your ingenuity and proficiency with Graffiti. This section explores some helpful tricks and techniques for using Memo Pad, beginning with some important information about becoming proficient with Graffiti.

NOTE 4,000 characters is roughly equivalent to 3/4 of a page (8 1/2" x 11") of text using 10-point font and single-spacing.

Get Comfortable

The first step to increasing your proficiency with Graffiti is to make sure you are as comfortable as possible using the PalmPilot. It's much easier learning how to play tennis if you have a graphite racquet and brand new tennis balls than it is with an old wooden badminton racquet and deflated balls. Make sure you have a stylus that you are comfortable using. If you are new to writing on a glass surface, you may want to place something with a paper-like texture over the Graffiti area to help simulate the surface friction you are familiar with when writing.

Cross makes a stylus refill for its line of rollerball pens. By purchasing this refill, you can use your favorite—and most comfortable—Cross pen with your PalmPilot, instead of the small nail-stylus that comes with the PalmPilot. Other pen manufacturers have followed suit—chances are there is a stylus refill for your favorite pen, no matter what make. Use Post-It paper or tape across the Graffiti pad to help create more of a paper feel.

TIP Check out the Web sites of Pilot Gear H.Q. (**www.pilotgear.com**), PDA Panache Corp. (**www.pdapanache.com**), and several pen manufacturers for stylus and other PDA writing aids.

Also check with your local retailer and look in the literature that came with your PalmPilot.

If possible, try out the stylus at a local office-supply retailer before buying it through a mail-order store.

Graffiti Proficiency

Learn Graffiti, and learn it well. That is the most important step in optimizing your use of the Memo Pad and other text-intensive applications. The more accurate you are when you enter characters, the less mistakes you will have to correct and the more time you will save. And, when you are jotting down information in front of a potential client or a business associate, you certainly want to avoid having to ask them to repeat the information because you are struggling with Graffiti.

Familiarity and practice are the keys to Graffiti proficiency. Take a good look through the PalmPilot's manual and memorize not only the letter and number strokes, but the special character and command strokes as well. Stick the "cheat sheet" sticker provided on the back of your PalmPilot so that you can refer to it whenever necessary. If your PalmPilot's case has room, carry the Graffiti quick-reference card with you as well.

TIP Save yourself some extra time to learn the basic characters and punctuation by ignoring the accent characters, which generally are used only in International languages.

Avoid the tendency to write small characters, which are harder for Graffiti to recognize. Write full-size characters within the Graffiti area. Also remember that Graffiti uses *strokes* to recognize characters; you can't leave the stylus against the Graffiti area—you must touch and lift for each character.

Use the 3Com Corporation's Giraffe game to test your Graffiti skills and to increase your speed. If you have a PalmPilot, Giraffe is already installed. If you have an earlier Pilot 1000 or 5000 model, you can install the game from the disks included with it.

NOTE Look in the PalmPilot Add-Ons directory for GIRAFFE.PRC. ■

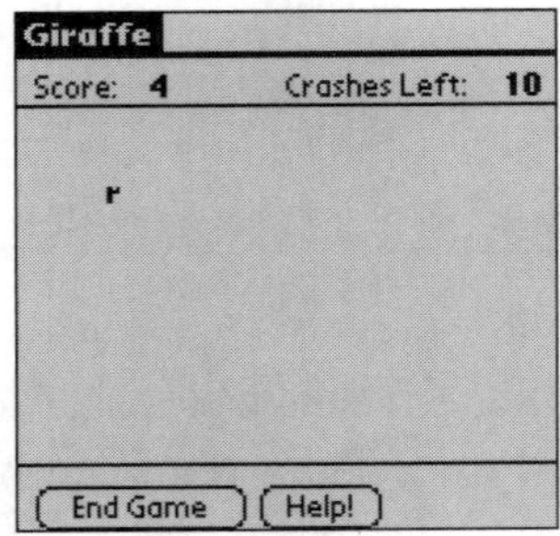

FIGURE 4.2
Giraffe is a fun way to practice your Graffiti skills.

PalmPilot users can also use the built-in Graffiti Help application to check on particular strokes. To activate Graffiti Help, use one of the following methods:

- Enter the Graffiti Help command (command stroke + G).
- Choose Graffiti from the application's Edit menu.
- Configure the upward stroke (starting in the Graffiti area and extending up outside of it) to activate Graffiti Help instead of using the Keyboard.

There are other, third-party Graffiti help applications available. The oldest and best is *GraffitiHelp* version 1.6 from Bill Kirby. Kirby's GraffitiHelp is very similar to 3Com Corporation's own Graffiti Help, showing normal, shift, extended, and accented characters. However, instead of paging down through the different character sets, you use the buttons at the bottom of the display to show the individual character sets.

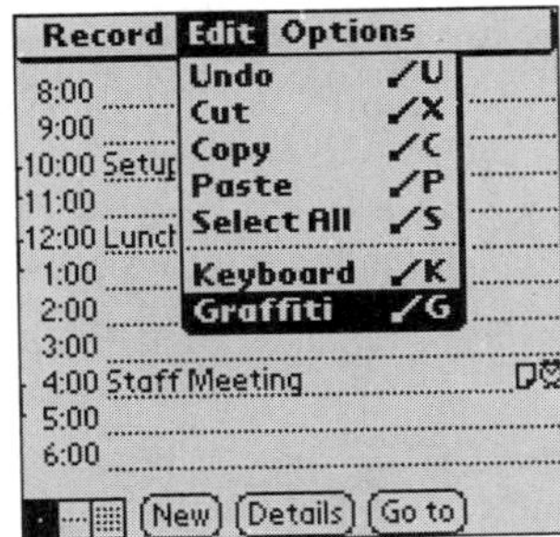

FIGURE 4.3
Graffiti Help is available from the Edit menu of most PalmPilot applications.

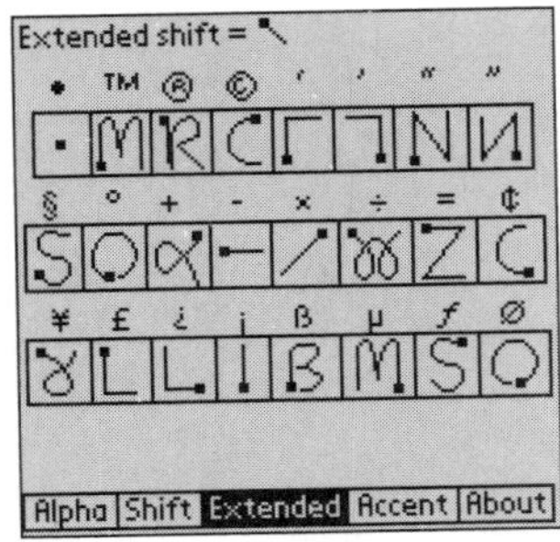

FIGURE 4.4
Graffiti Help helps you remember those seldom-used characters.

Alternate Text Entry

There are several other methods you can use to quickly and accurately enter text into Memo Pad, as explained in the following sections.

Use PalmPilot's Keyboard The easiest, though far from the quickest, method for entering text is to use the PalmPilot's built-in keyboard to "touch-tap" your text.

To activate the keyboard, use one of the following methods:

- Enter the Keyboard command (command stroke + "K").
- Choose Keyboard from the Edit menu.
- Draw a vertical stroke up and out of the Graffiti area.

FIGURE 4.5
You can use the PalmPilot's keyboard to enter text instead of Graffiti.

TIP If you have a PalmPilot, you can also activate the keyboard by tapping the small dot in the lower-left corner of the Graffiti area. This alleviates the need to use the vertical stroke shortcut to the keyboard, making it available to be used for other purposes.

Using Predefined Shortcuts Another method for entering text into the Memo Pad is to have the text predefined as a shortcut. When you notice that you are consistently entering the same text over and over in your memos, take a moment to define a shortcut for that text. This brief step will save you much time and effort in writing future memos. Key candidates for shortcuts are the current date and time, words repeatedly used in the title of memos (such as "staff meeting" or particular product names), and names of friends or coworkers.

NOTE Shortcuts are defined from within the Preferences application. To define a shortcut, you need to indicate a few characters to identify the shortcut and the text to be entered when the shortcut is used. Then, to use a shortcut, simply enter the shortcut character, followed by the identifying text. See your PalmPilot's manual for more information on defining and using shortcuts.

TIP You can enter the date stamp or time stamp (current date and time) at the beginning of your own shortcuts. Enter **@DS** for the date stamp, **@TS** for the time stamp, and **@DTS** for the date and time stamp. Note that these stamps must be entered at the beginning of your shortcut—they will not be recognized anywhere else inside the shortcut. Also note that you need to use the @ symbol instead of the shortcut stroke.

Remember, too, that the PalmPilot has rudimentary cut-and-paste functionality. This can save you from having to reenter lengthy text that is available in another memo or application. Simply highlight the appropriate text, wherever it may be, and enter either the Cut or Copy command (command stroke + X or C), switch to the destination application, and enter the Paste command (command stroke + P).

TIP PalmPilot users can quickly enter names and numbers from the Address Book by using the Phone Lookup feature from the Options menu.

Using the PalmPilot Desktop and HotSync Don't forget that you can also enter text into the PalmPilot desktop and then HotSync it to your PalmPilot. Using a full-sized keyboard is much easier for lengthy documents, but you sacrifice the portability of the PalmPilot.

NOTE See your PalmPilot manual for more information about the PalmPilot Desktop and HotSync.

Devise Your Own Shorthand

Another way to write more is actually to write less. Devise shorthand ways of writing common words and phrases and then use these devices consistently. Abbreviate words, invent short phrases, use symbols. For example, consider the following examples shown in Table 4.1.

Table 4.1 Shorthand Examples

Shorthand	Meaning
mtg	meeting
chk/w	check with
appt	appointment
???	question, find out about
!!!	extremely important

Everyone has a style of shorthand they use when writing or taking notes. Try to emulate your written shorthand as much as possible, and use your Memo Pad shorthand when you write on normal paper to stay in practice.

Attaching Notes

Almost every PalmPilot application has the capability to attach textual notes to individual records. These notes resemble a Memo Pad document, but appear in other applications; they cannot be accessed from Memo Pad directly.

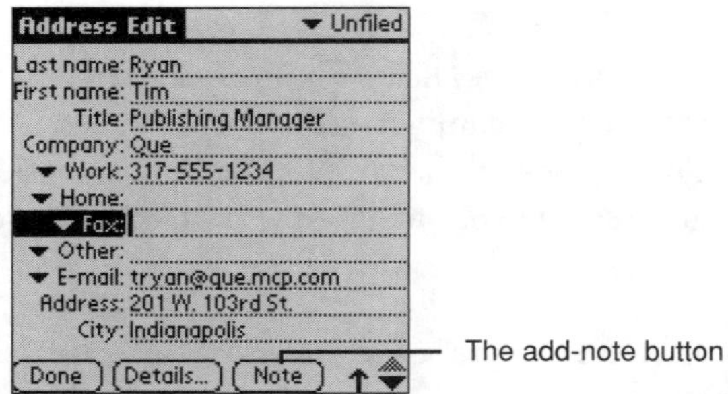

FIGURE 4.6
With the Address Book, you can attach notes to records—use them to store additional information, such as the names of a person's family members or directions to their home or business.

These small notes can be very helpful when used in conjunction with their corresponding data. For example, you can enter directions for a hard-to-find client site in a note attached to that client's Address Book entry, or you can attach an agenda to the weekly staff meeting reminder in the Date Book.

NOTE Unfortunately, you are confined to using Memo Pad to create and edit these notes in PalmPilot applications—you cannot install or configure a third-party editor to do so. However, some third-party applications have their own note-editing features that do not use Memo Pad.

TIP If you use a desktop computer, you are probably used to being able to embed different types of data in different applications. For example, you probably have placed a spreadsheet in a word-processing document, or vice versa.

Although you can't really do this with the PalmPilot, you can place markers in one application that point to data in another application. For example, when referencing a client in a Memo Pad document, use an abbreviated form of their name. You can then quickly copy and paste the abbreviation into the Find dialog to help locate other memos or address entries for the client.

If you are placing the related data in another application, add the name of the application before the data. For example, to reference a rendering of a product logo in DinkyPad, you might use:

```
dinky:  Jake Speed Logo
```

More Text Space

The PalmPilot was designed to take notes, not write novels. You might be surprised how much information fits into the 4,000-character limit of Memo Pad. However, if you find yourself exceeding this limit on a regular basis, you will want to find an additional text display or editing application. The following sections cover some of your options for text editing.

Pilot DOC

Pilot DOC, by Rick Bram, is an application that enables you to view text documents that were compressed using a scheme designed by Pat Beirne. This compression scheme can compress documents by as much as 50 percent. Pilot DOC can handle compressed documents of any size, providing you have enough free memory.

NOTE You need more free memory to actually view a document in Pilot DOC than you need just to store it. Pilot DOC decompresses the document before displaying it, causing the document to eat up more memory.

Note that Pilot DOC is only a reader; you cannot edit the displayed text. This makes it ideal for reference material, but impractical for information that changes on a frequent basis. Many PalmPilot users even install electronic novels on their PalmPilot and use DOC to read them.

NOTE Most of the electronic novels available consist of public-domain works such as Shakespeare. For a more contemporary novel, check out *BuffaloGirls*, a work in progress from Kristen Brennan. The full novel can be found on the Internet at **www.jitterbug.com/pages/buffalo.html** or on this book's companion CD.

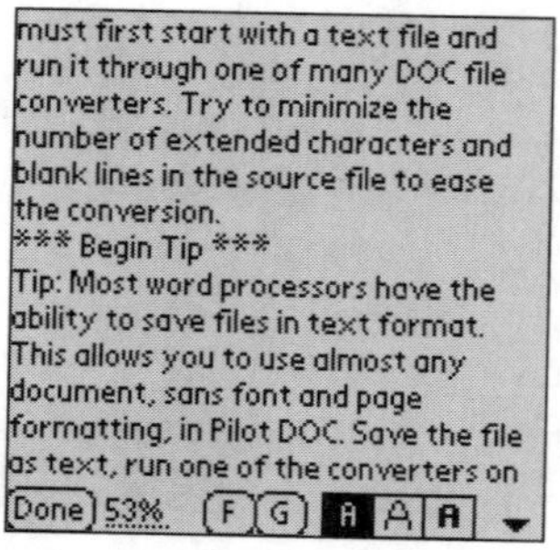

must first start with a text file and
run it through one of many DOC file
converters. Try to minimize the
number of extended characters and
blank lines in the source file to ease
the conversion.
*** Begin Tip ***
Tip: Most word processors have the
ability to save files in text format.
This allows you to use almost any
document, sans font and page
formatting, in Pilot DOC. Save the file
as text, run one of the converters on
Done 53% F G A A A

FIGURE 4.7
Use Pilot DOC for easy reading of documents larger than Memo Pad's 4,000 character limit.

Pilot DOC has many features that make browsing and reading documents easy, as shown in Table 4.2.

Table 4.2 Pilot DOC Features

Feature	Use
Find	Quickly search for text within the current document or all documents in DOC.
Find Again	Search for the next occurrence of the specified text.
Go	Go to the top, bottom, or to a percentage of the current document. (Also allows jumping to predefined bookmarks—see Bookmarks.)
Bookmarks	User-defined positions within the text that can be accessed by using the Go feature. Handy for marking your progress in a book or for creating a table of contents in a long document.
Multiple Fonts	View text in the normal, bold, or large font.
Copy Text	Copy highlighted text to Paste in another application.
Timer	A variable-speed auto-scroll feature for DOC. Configure it to scroll at your reading speed to alleviate the need to manually scroll the text as you read.

Pilot DOC documents are transferred to the PalmPilot as separate PRC or PDB (PalmPilot Resource or PalmPilot Database) files. Pilot DOC itself is installed as a 25K PRC.

To create a file for Pilot DOC, you must first start with a text file and run it through one of many DOC file converters. Try to minimize the number of extended characters and blank lines in the source file to ease the conversion.

TIP Most word processors have the capability to save files in text format. This allows you to use almost any document, without font and page formatting, in Pilot DOC. Save the file as text, run one of the converters on it, and then HotSync it to your PalmPilot.

Rick Bram has a basic Pilot DOC converter called *MakeDoc* that runs at a DOS prompt. This no-frills approach enables you to quickly convert a file for Pilot DOC use. Simply enter the name of the text document, the desired name of the DOC file, and the title of the document. The result is a PRC or PDB that is ready for HotSync.

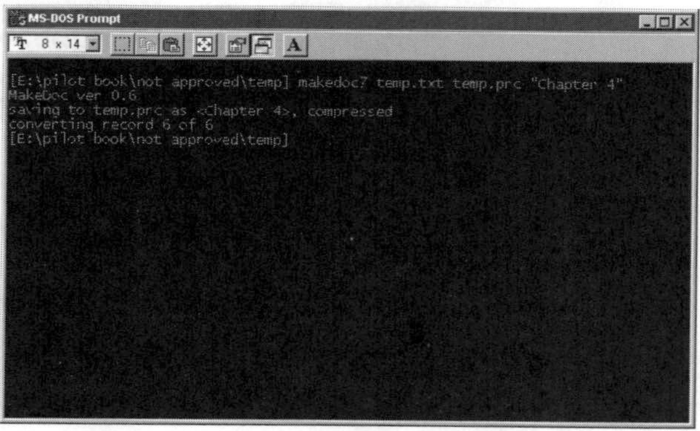

FIGURE 4.8
MakeDoc quickly converts text files to DOC files.

Mark Pierce has taken the conversion program one step further by developing a Windows 95-compatible version—*MakeDoc for Windows.* This converter offers many additional options for converting text and has the benefit of using common dialogs because it runs in Windows 95. MakeDoc for Windows also offers an auto-install feature that will automatically mark the new DOC file for HotSync.

SuperPad

SuperPad, by Alexander S. Hinds, is a Memo Pad replacement that is capable of displaying and editing large Memo Pad documents. In addition to breaking the 4,000-character barrier, SuperPad adds the capability to encrypt memos with a user-definable password and uses on-the-fly compression to minimize the size of memos.

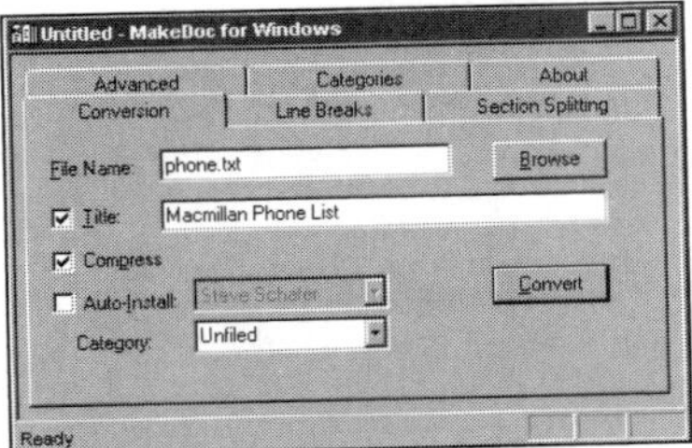

FIGURE 4.9
MakeDoc for Windows adds many configuration options for converting files and is much easier to use in the Windows environment.

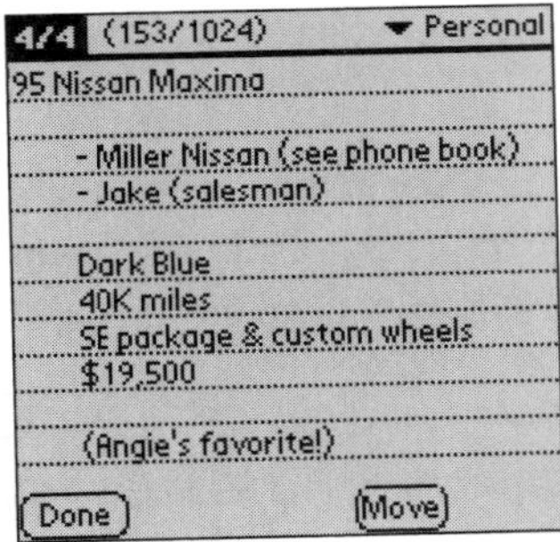

FIGURE 4.10
SuperPad breaks the 4,000-character Memo Pad limit while preserving all of Memo Pad's features.

Besides a few extra buttons and display options, SuperPad looks and functions just like Memo Pad. You can use it as a direct Memo Pad replacement if you want.

NOTE You must specify the largest size of memo within SuperPad (in segments of 1,000 characters). Be careful not to start with too large of a value; if you need to scale back at some point, you will lose the ability to edit documents larger than the lower value you set.

TIP Use SilkHack or the PalmPilot button preferences to redefine a button on your PalmPilot to access SuperPad directly.

> **CAUTION** Large memos created with SuperPad will HotSync to your computer, but you can only edit the first 4,000 characters with the PalmPilot desktop.

Non-Text Information

There are many ways to represent data; plain text is only one of them. The native PalmPilot applications are suited only for plain text. However, there are a handful of third-party applications designed for other data collection and display.

Graphical Information

One of the first add-on applications Pilot 1000 users started requesting was a way to draw by using the Pilot's touch screen. Using the full power of the touch screen, maps could be drawn, product prototypes sketched out, and other graphical information represented.

> **TIP** Graphic data takes a lot of memory. This section will highlight the memory requirements for each of the applications and their corresponding data so that you can factor in these memory requirements when choosing an application(s) to use.

DinkyPad To fulfill the need for touch-screen drawing, Edward Keyes created DinkyPad. DinkyPad, the first full-featured drawing application for the Pilot 1000, enables you to draw lines, circles, and rectangles in five different pen sizes on a canvas 2,040 pixels long. An eraser function lets you quickly remove mistakes, and all drawings are compressed to save valuable memory.

Each drawing is saved as a separate record in the DinkyPad database. The selection list of DinkyPad shows a small thumbnail of the drawing. Also, each drawing can be annotated with a line of text for easy identification.

The DinkyPad application takes up about 21K of memory, while each drawing occupies up to 2K. Shortly after DinkyPad was made available, Stu Slack created DinkyView, a DinkyPad drawing viewer for the PC. DinkyView also allows other drawings to be imported, spawning the online exchange of graphics for DinkyPad.

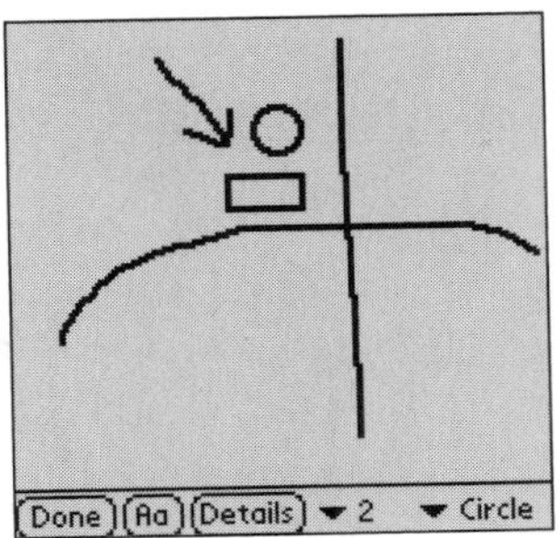

FIGURE 4.11
DinkyPad enables you to draw on the PalmPilot's screen to store graphical information.

NOTE At the time of this writing, DinkyPad drawings could be HotSynced to the PalmPilot only with Generic Conduit 1.1. This version of the Conduit only supports HotSync version 1.1, so PalmPilot users will not be able to HotSync drawings from the desktop until a new version of the Generic Conduit is available.

Among the most popular DinkyPad drawings are scans of Dilbert and other popular cartoons.

CAUTION It's a bad idea, and usually illegal, to scan and distribute other people's work without their permission.

NOTE DinkyPad remains the most popular drawing application for the PalmPilot, probably due to its longevity and desktop application support.

Other Drawing Applications For a long time, DinkyPad was the only PalmPilot drawing application available. Recently, another whole crop of drawing applications has appeared online.

Doodle Roger E. Critchlow, Jr.'s Doodle application offers many pen and ink styles and effects. Instead of providing a standard PalmPilot database, Doodle stores its drawings in pages, much like a scratch pad.

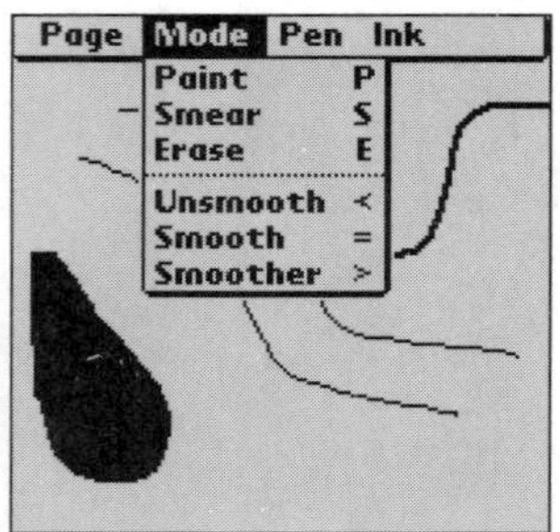

FIGURE 4.12
Doodle provides several types of pens and inks for creative drawing.

Doodle's strength is in its pens and inks. It is easier to create actual drawings in Doodle, but the inability to easily create circles and polygons makes it harder to construct technical drawings.

The Doodle application uses about 5K of system RAM, with each page taking another 3.5K.

Scribble Scribble, by Andrew Howlett, is the simplest of the drawing applications available. It simply enables you to write freeform lines on the PalmPilot's screen and one line of text at the bottom of the screen. There is only one pen size and limited commands (Delete Page and Copy Text), but Scribble uses only 5K total RAM, drawing and all.

Scratch Pad Scratch Pad, by Eric Kenslow, is similar to Scribble but allows you to save multiple pages of drawings. Like Scribble, Scratch Pad has only one pen size, but adds an eraser for fine corrections.

Scratch Pad occupies about 5K, with an additional 4K for each additional drawing added.

FIGURE 4.13
Scribble is among the most simple drawing programs, allowing only one page of scribbling.

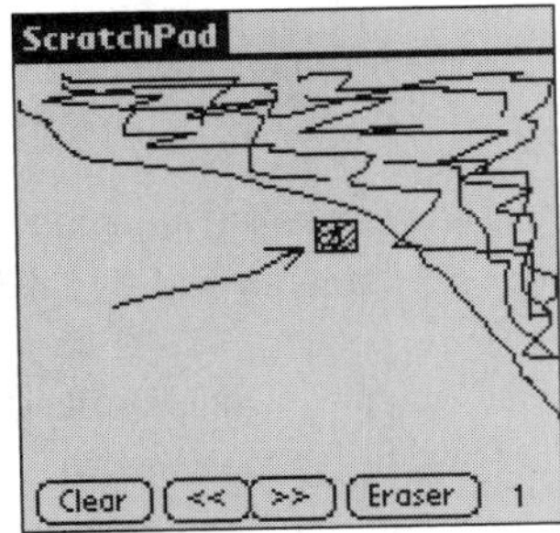

FIGURE 4.14
Scratch Pad is fairly limited in capability, but does support multiple pages for multiple drawings.

QPaint QPaint, by Mikita Yasuda, is perhaps the most functional drawing application for the PalmPilot. Providing a good mix of tools and features, QPaint is much more like the paint programs found on desktop computers.

QPaint offers the widest range of tools, including the standard pen and eraser, several prefabricated shapes (circle, rectangle, and rounded rectangle), a paint fill tool with several textures, and even a text tool for adding text to your drawings.

FIGURE 4.15
Similar to many desktop computer paint programs, QPaint is the most capable drawing program available for the PalmPilot.

Each drawing is stored in a separate record in the QPaint database and the browse screen displays large thumbnails for easy identification of your drawings.

All of QPaint's capabilities come with a price—the application takes 14K of memory with each drawing occupying an additional 3–4K.

NOTE The lack of desktop support is perhaps QPaint's only shortcoming. If you need a feature-rich drawing application but don't need to back up your drawings to your desktop, choose to load QPaint on your PalmPilot.

PalmDraw A recent entry in the PalmPilot drawing-application category is PalmDraw, by Bradley Keith Goodman. PalmDraw is unique in the following ways:

- It draws vector (line-based) shapes, including bezier curves.
- Each shape is an object that can be resized and moved independently of other shapes.
- Your drawings can be printed directly to a PostScript printer or transferred to the PalmPilot's Memo Pad in PostScript format.

There is also a conversion application for PalmDraw that allows your drawings to be converted to Windows Meta Files (WMF) after being HotSynced to the desktop.

NOTE At the time of this writing, PalmDraw was a beta release and its capabilities were still growing. Check out the PalmDraw Web site for more information: **www.oai.com/bkg/Pilot/PalmDraw**.

PhotoAlbum PhotoAlbum, from OBE Systems, is a display-only application that can display true grayscale images on the PalmPilot's display screen. A shareware application for Windows translates bitmap (BMP) files into PhotoAlbum records that can be HotSynced to your PalmPilot for display.

Although PhotoAlbum is only a display application, its use of the PalmPilot's display is phenomenal—you must see it to believe it!

NOTE The PhotoAlbum viewer is free; download it from OBE Systems' Web site at **members.aol.com/PilotPhoto/index.htm**. However, the Windows-translation utility is $15 US and can be ordered only via mail.

Data Collection Forms

Occasionally you might find yourself collecting data with your PalmPilot. Instead of laboring to find a means to utilize Memo Pad for this task, take a look at *Pilot Forms* from Pendragon Software.

Pilot Forms enables you to define complex forms using graphical elements such as pop-up lists and check boxes. These forms can then be used to collect data in individual records, which in turn can be HotSynced to the desktop and imported into a database for advanced manipulation.

Pilot Forms uses a Windows-based WYSIWYG editor to build the forms, which are then HotSynced to the PalmPilot. The PalmPilot-based forms program utilizes the form template to collect data in database format that can be exported as a delimited file to the desktop.

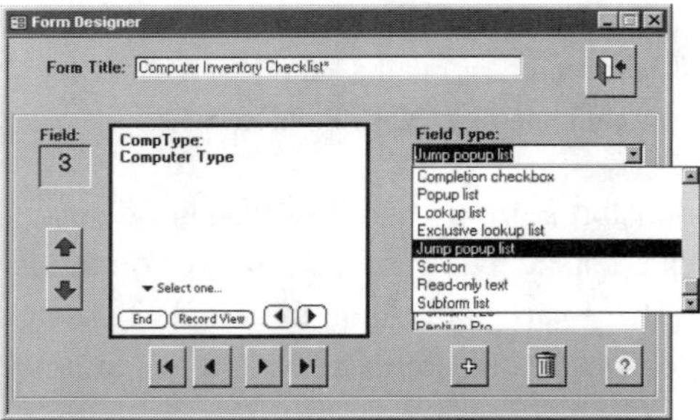

FIGURE 4.16
Pilot Forms allows you to collect data on your PalmPilot using custom forms.

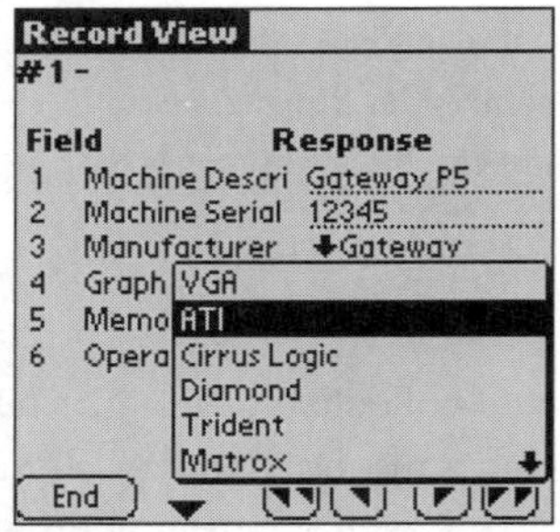

FIGURE 4.17
The PalmPilot-based program collects and displays data using the custom-built form.

Whether you survey potential customers in their homes, track scientific data in a laboratory, or interview patients in a medical facility, Pilot Forms will enable you to utilize your PalmPilot for this task.

NOTE Pilot Forms is commercial software. The full package currently runs $49.95, plus shipping and handling, and can be ordered from Pendragon's Web site: **www.webfayre.com/pilot/**.

CHAPTER 5

Staying on Top of Finances

Besides managing your schedule and your contacts, the PalmPilot can also help you monitor and manage your finances. The standard PalmPilot comes with a full-featured calculator, but it is the third-party applications that lend the most support for managing finances on your PalmPilot. This chapter will examine these resources and how they can be used to help you better control your budget, spending, and accounting.

NOTE Automatic banking through use of your PalmPilot is not yet possible, but may be right around the corner. Current applications can use data that is compatible with desktop applications, such as Quicken, and interface to online services. Look for more connectivity software to be available in the near future!

Financial Calculations

The most basic financial feature of the PalmPilot is its ability to operate as a calculator, whether just the basic calculator included with the PalmPilot or one of the powerful third-party calculator applications. This section will highlight the various calculator options currently available for your PalmPilot.

PalmPilot Calculator

The calculator that comes with the PalmPilot is useful for basic calculations, but is fairly limited in scope. There are a couple of features that you can exploit to make the Calculator more practical in day-to-day use.

Recent Calculations Under the Options menu, the Recent Calculations feature allows you to view the last few calculations you have made, much like reviewing the tape of an adding machine.

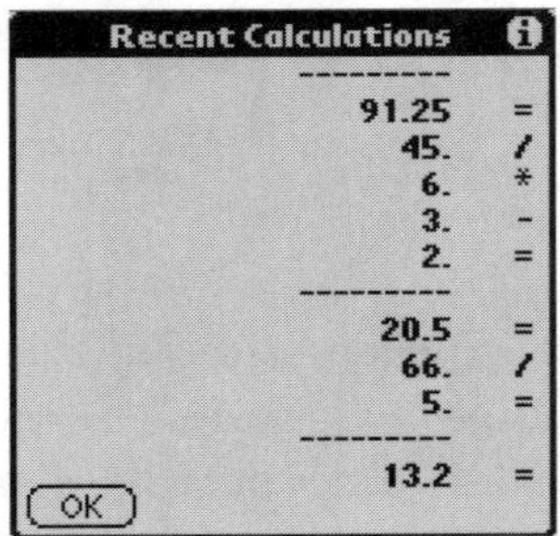

FIGURE 5.1
Forget how you arrived at that total? The Recent Calculations feature can come to your rescue.

NOTE Unfortunately, you can only *look* at the calculations, not repeat, cut/paste, or otherwise work with them.

Copy/Paste These two options enable you to copy the total out of the Calculator or paste a number into it. Using these features, you can import numbers from other applications for calculations and paste the results into applications.

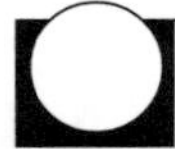

TIP The original Calculator that came with the Pilot 1000 and 5000 models was prone to rounding errors, causing mistakes in calculations. U.S. Robotics quickly released an update to the calculator, *SlimCalc 2.0*. Although the fix takes up RAM instead of the Pilot 1000's and 5000's ROM, it does fix the rounding errors. You can quickly find out if you have the update by looking at the size and shape of the "+" key. If the key is small and square, it is the original Calculator. If the key is longer and rectangular, then it is the updated Calculator.

Call 3Com Corporation to receive the update or download it from your favorite online PalmPilot resource. The small PRC file can be installed through HotSync like any other program.

Abacus Financial Calculator

The Abacus Financial Calculator, by DovCom, is a full-featured RPN (Reverse Polish Notation) financial calculator that is based on the HP-12C calculator from Hewlett-Packard.

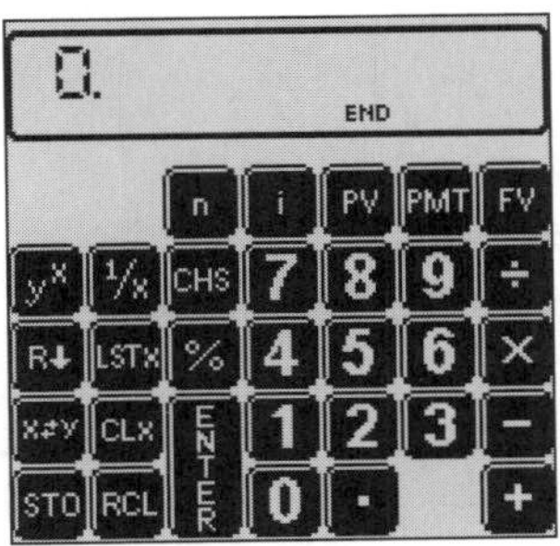

FIGURE 5.2

Abacus' layout and operation emulates an HP-12C calculator.

The layout and design of the calculator should be familiar to anyone who has used a similar HP calculator. The RPN operation is easier to use for scientific and financial calculations.

CalCOOLator

CalCOOLator, by Fabio Vitali, is another calculator for the PalmPilot. The main benefit of this calculator is its dual-field entry system. This allows you to enter the calculations in one field and view the results in the other. You can then edit the calculation field, changing the result, without having to re-key the entire formula.

CalCOOLator also has three types of grouping parenthesis for setting precedence in your calculations, and three memory locations in which to store calculations. Its unique design might take some getting used to, but if you perform frequent calculations with several variables, you will find it very useful.

MathPad

MathPad, by Rick Huebner, is a powerful equation-solving application. Entering an expression or equation is like entering text in Memo Pad; simply use Graffiti or the Keyboard. You can include functions for operators, exponentiation, factorials, bitwise operations (AND, OR, NOT, and XOR), bit shifts, integer or modulo division, absolute value, and square root.

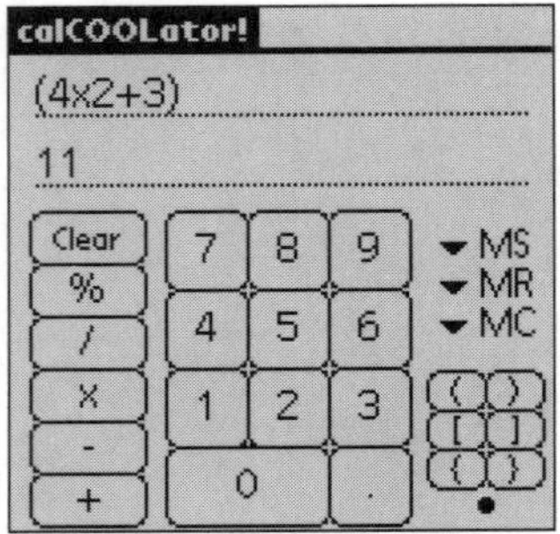

FIGURE 5.3
CalCOOLator may not look like much, but its unique two-register design makes it a powerful tool indeed.

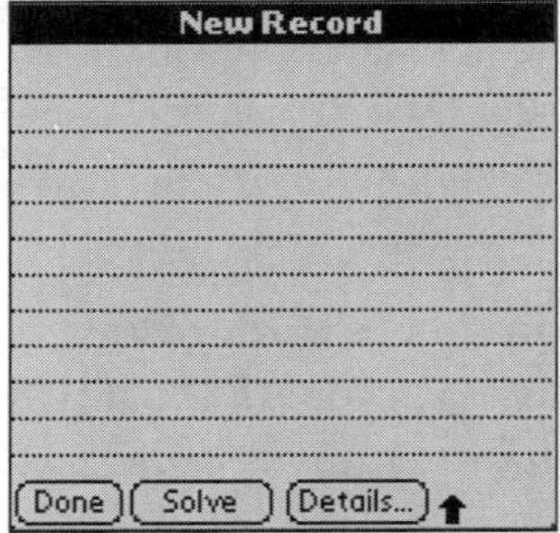

FIGURE 5.4
MathPad looks a bit like Memo Pad but solves algebraic expressions and equations.

Tap the Solve key to have MathPad solve the expression or equation for you. For example, if you enter "3+2=", tapping solve will return "5." Likewise, a more complex equation like "(3+18)/7=y+2" will display "1" for the variable "y."

When solving equations, you need to provide a space for MathPad to display the value of the variable, as well as the equation. In the example above, you would need to enter "y:" on another line. Pressing Solve will put the value "1" after the colon on that line.

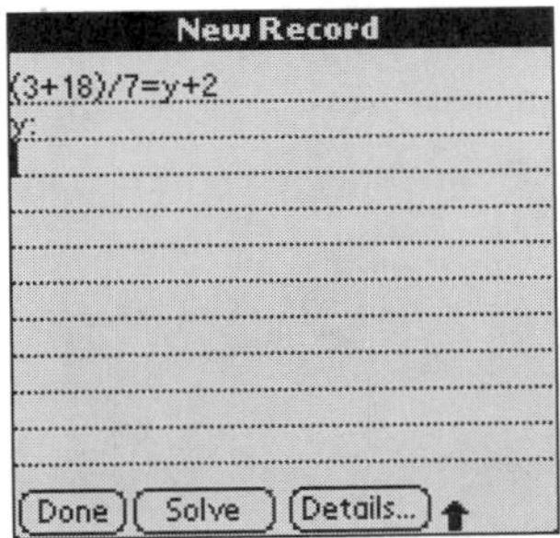

FIGURE 5.5
Equations require variable lines for output.

NOTE MathPad *requires* OS 2.x due to its reliance on new arithmetic functions that are provided in the new ROM.

RPN

RPN, by Russell Y. Webb, was one of the first third-party calculators for the PalmPilot and continues to be a favorite. RPN borrows its name from its calculation method, Reverse Polish Notation. RPN includes several trigonometric functions, a forty-element stack, nine user variables, and it offers scientific, engineering, or fixed display.

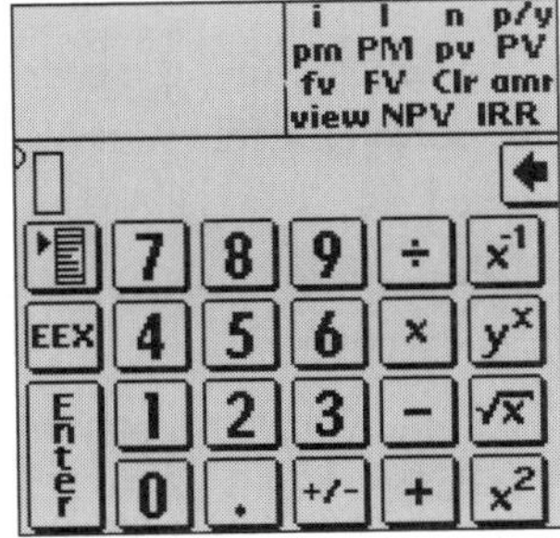

FIGURE 5.6
RPN is a full-featured RPN-style calculator.

However, what makes RPN unique and most useful is its scripting feature. This feature enables you to import new functions into the calculator, giving it new capabilities. RPN comes with several functions, including Scientific Functions, Logs and Powers, Unit Conversion Utilities, Day and Time functions, and a rudimentary Checkbook.

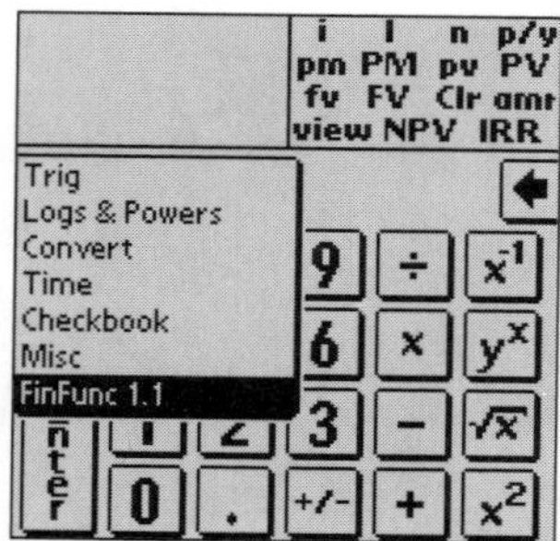

FIGURE 5.7
RPN's scripting capability enables you to easily extend its capability beyond those that it comes with.

Other scripts have been developed for RPN by other people. For example, *Air 2.0*, by P. Csurgay, includes:

Script	Use
WorldTime	A utility for determining the time anywhere in the world.
CurrencyEx	A utility for determining the currency exchange between twelve currencies of your choice.
Timers	Time an event or set a countdown to time when dinner is ready.
CountDown	Check how many days remain until a particular date.
PianoKeyb	Play, record, and play back melodies on an electronic piano.
MasterMind	Play a game of MasterMind.

FinFunctions, by Benjamin Cukier, is a set of financial functions for RPN, including all major financial operations and calculations.

NOTE RPN occupies about 36K of system RAM. Each additional script package takes more RAM accordingly. Air takes about 5K and FinFunctions takes under 1K.

To add scripts to RPN, you either load the script via HotSync (if the script has been compiled as a PRC) or use the PalmPilot desktop to import the textual script as a Memo and cut and paste it into RPN.

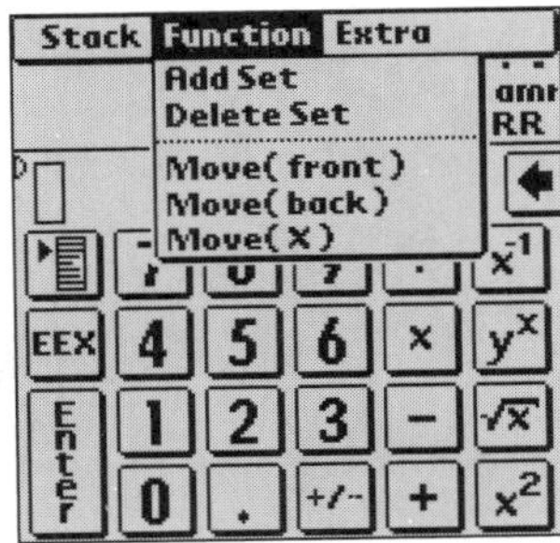

FIGURE 5.8
The Add Set option imports new scripts from the PalmPilot's Clipboard.

LoanCalc

LoanCalc, by Jerry Wang, is a simple program that is used to calculate the monthly payment and schedule for a loan, when given the amount of the loan, interest rate, and length of the loan (in years).

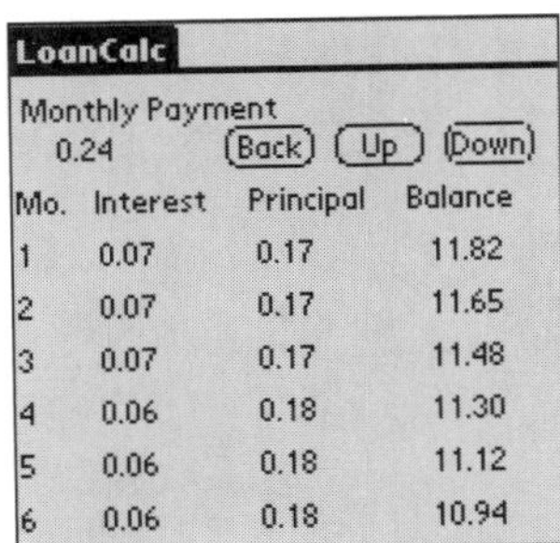

FIGURE 5.9
LoanCalc quickly calculates the payment and schedule of a loan when provided a few variables.

LoanCalc is valuable for anyone who has to quickly calculate the specifics of paying back a loan, such as when shopping for a car or real estate.

NOTE LoanCalc is a CASL program, requiring the CASL Runtime program (28K), which is included with LoanCalc. See Chapter 9, "Developing PalmPilot Software," for more information about CASL.

MoneyCalc

MoneyCalc, by Tan Kok Mun, is a collection of BASIC programs for calculating various loans, leases, and other financial obligations. MoneyCalc includes the following:

- An Amortization Schedule
- Car Leasing Calculations
- An Interest Calculator
- A Lease/Rent Calculator
- A Loan/Mortgage Calculator
- A Saving/Insurance Calculator
- A Sinking Fund Calculator

Each program requires that you enter a few variables for the calculation to be completed. Like LoanCalc, MoneyCalc is useful for anyone who regularly needs to compute financial obligations, such as loans and leases.

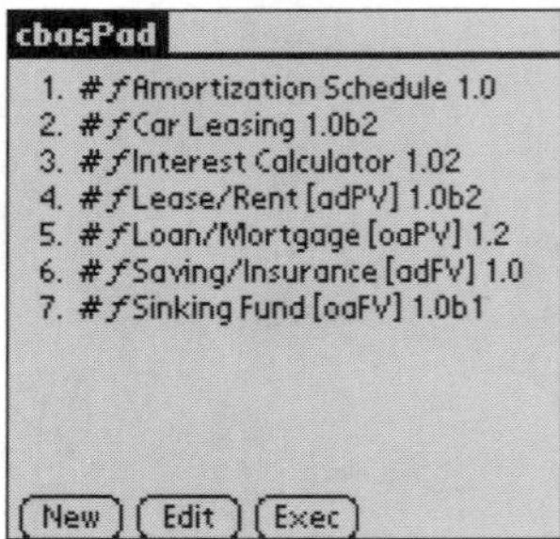

FIGURE 5.10
MoneyCalc can answer several financial questions with its set of cbasPad programs.

NOTE MoneyCalc requires cbasPad, a small BASIC interpreter by Ron Nicholson, modeled after Chipmunk BASIC. See Chapter 9, "Developing PalmPilot Software," for more information about cbasPad.

Tracking Expenses

After basic arithmetic calculations, the base level of using your PalmPilot for financial tracking and management is simply tracking money. If you take your PalmPilot with you on trips and business errands, you can use it to track every expense as you travel. You can use the OS 2.x Expense application or another third-party application to track every dollar you spend, and what it is spent on.

TIP The secret to successful expense tracking with the PalmPilot is, of course, to keep it with you and to use it. Take it with you to restaurants, meetings, and even to put gas in your rental car. Enter every business expense you need to track and HotSync your data to your desktop to help prepare your expense reports and to further analyze your expenses.

OS 2.x Expense

PalmPilot OS 2.x includes a basic expense-tracking program. This program allows you to enter expenses into individual records, categorized by type, and filed by category. The fields provided include one to enter how the payment was made (cash, credit card, etc.) and one to enter the type of currency paid. You also can enter where the expense occurred, by vendor and city, and append a note for further information.

You can use the PalmPilot Desktop (2.x) to HotSync your expenses to the desktop and export them into Excel format for further calculations and reporting.

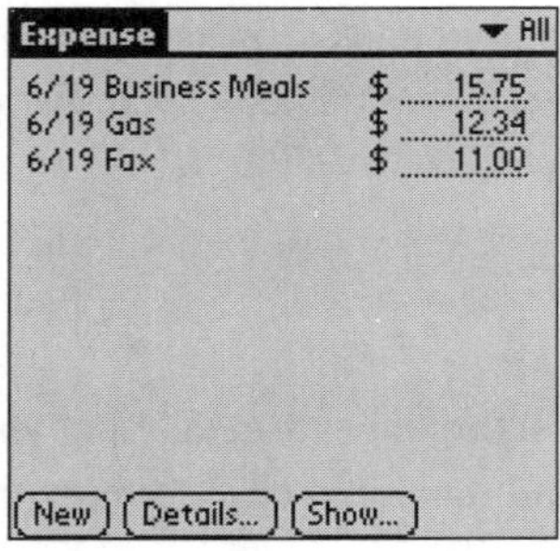

FIGURE 5.11
The PalmPilot's Expense application can track your expenses when you travel.

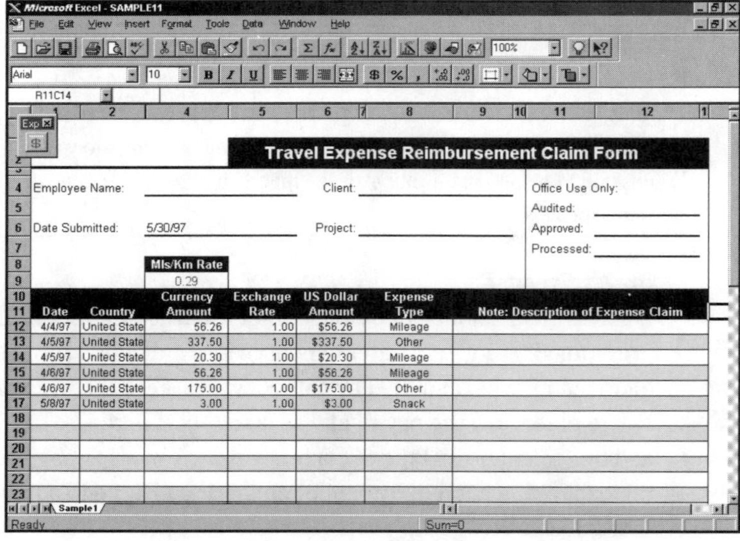

Travel Expense Reimbursement Claim Form

Employee Name:
Client:
Office Use Only:
Audited:
Date Submitted: 5/30/97
Project:
Approved:
Processed:

Mls/Km Rate
0.29

Date	Country	Currency Amount	Exchange Rate	US Dollar Amount	Expense Type	Note: Description of Expense Claim
4/4/97	United State	56.26	1.00	$56.26	Mileage	
4/5/97	United State	337.50	1.00	$337.50	Other	
4/5/97	United State	20.30	1.00	$20.30	Mileage	
4/6/97	United State	56.26	1.00	$56.26	Mileage	
4/6/97	United State	175.00	1.00	$175.00	Other	
5/8/97	United State	3.00	1.00	$3.00	Snack	

FIGURE 5.12
Several templates included with the PalmPilot Desktop 2.x makes your expense reports shine.

ExpenseReporter

ExpenseReporter, by iambic Software, is a third-party expense-tracking application much like the PalmPilot's Expense application. However, iambic adds a few bells and whistles to its expense application:

- Three user-configurable fields to enter payment, payee, and location information. Each field can be filled in by selecting from a list or adding a new entry—which then gets added to the appropriate list.
- Codes to track account information can be added to each of the fields—tracking who paid, whom was paid, and what was paid for.
- Daily totals of expenses.
- A Mileage calculator that uses odometer values.
- Multiple currency values with conversion, to which you can add your own values and conversion rates.

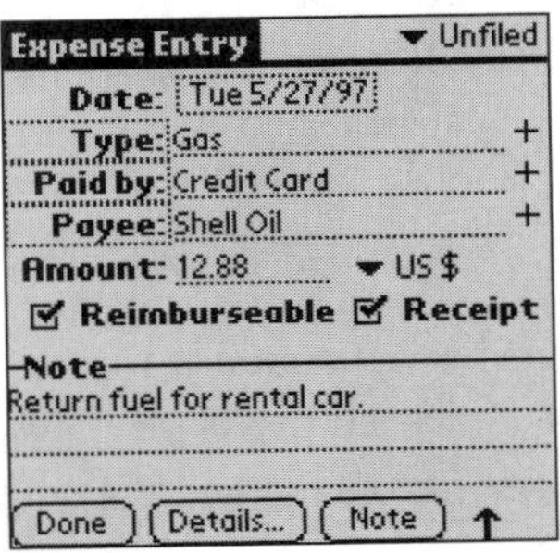

FIGURE 5.13
ExpenseReporter has some bells and whistles above and beyond the basic Expense application included with the PalmPilot.

ExpenseReporter can HotSync your expense data to the desktop in a tab-delimited text file that can then be imported into your favorite spreadsheet.

Hourz

Hourz, by Andrew Zaeske, is another program that can be used to track finances. Hourz is limited to tracking consulting times and fees, but it excels at it. You can enter a date, time range, rate of pay, and any additional notes necessary.

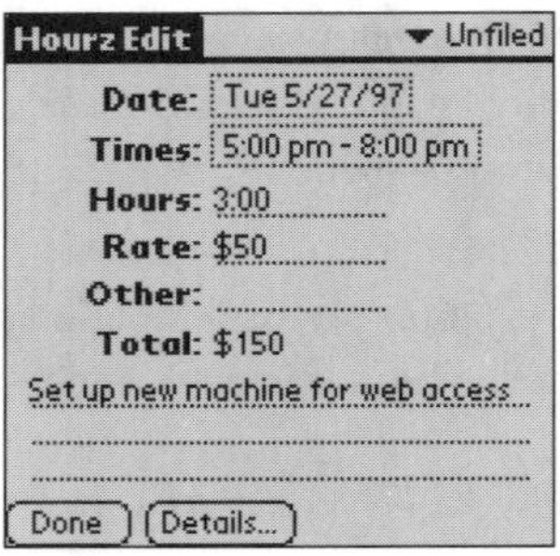

FIGURE 5.14
Although limited to tracking time, Hourz is one of the best applications for doing so.

Hourz is shareware—registration entitles you to export your records to the desktop in tab-delimited format, ready for import into your favorite spreadsheet.

Total Money Management

So far, this chapter has covered the basics of money tracking and management using the PalmPilot. However, there are a few applications for the PalmPilot that take these tasks further, giving you total money management on your PalmPilot.

These programs offer more than simplistic money accounting and calculations; they can be used by anyone who needs to manage actual monetary accounts on-the-go.

PilotMoney

PilotMoney, by StingerSoft, is an electronic bookkeeper. You can create up to sixteen accounts and track every credit and debit in each account. Every transaction can be marked as outstanding or cleared, allowing you to quickly reconcile each account.

You can include a custom or preconfigured description for each transaction to help identify it later. You can also mark a transaction to reoccur every week, two weeks, month, or end of the month. This allows for quick entry of transactions such as rent and regular paychecks. You also can add a textual note to each transaction for any details that don't fit in the predefined fields.

FIGURE 5.15
PilotMoney is a complete solution for tracking financial accounts with the PalmPilot.

NOTE Version 1.58 of PilotMoney for PalmPilot OS 2.x adds the Lookup feature to its note field, allowing quick entry of records in the Address Book.

PilotMoney also has several built-in reports to view your data, including Ending Balances, Unpaid Checks, and Reconciled Balance. The version for OS 2.x will even inform you if an account will be overdrawn and will show you the offending transactions.

A partner program, *Money Exporter*, enables you to export your records in Quicken, Excel, or MemoPad format. In Quicken and Excel, the data is exported to your desktop computer via the PalmPilot's serial port, whereas the MemoPad option sends the data to the PalmPilot's Memo Pad, where the data is then HotSynced to the desktop.

FIGURE 5.16
Money Exporter will export selected records in several different formats for use on your desktop machine.

STAYING ON TOP OF FINANCES

The PilotMoney application only takes 35K and is the ultimate application for tracking financial accounts with your PalmPilot.

QMate

QMate, by Steve Dakin, brings Quicken to your PalmPilot. Using a database system similar to Quicken's own, QMate enables you to create multiple accounts in which you can enter credits and debits, complete with a textual memo and Quicken-compatible category.

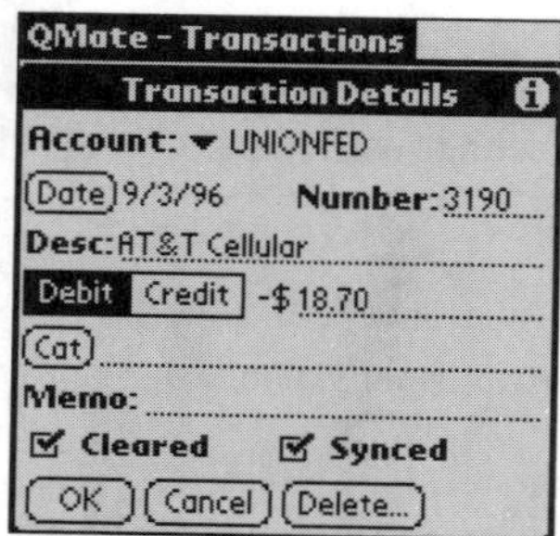

FIGURE 5.17
Quicken users will feel right at home in QMate.

Each transaction has a cleared check box for reconciliation, and the database can be imported and exported to your desktop machine during each HotSync. You can export categories and records from Quicken for the PalmPilot, or import them into Quicken from the PalmPilot.

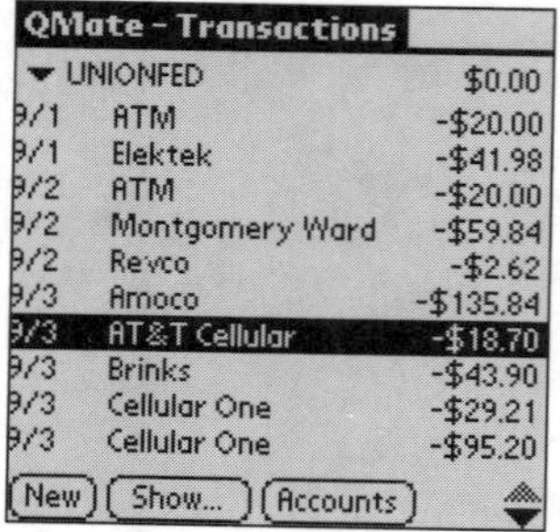

FIGURE 5.18
Use QMate by itself...

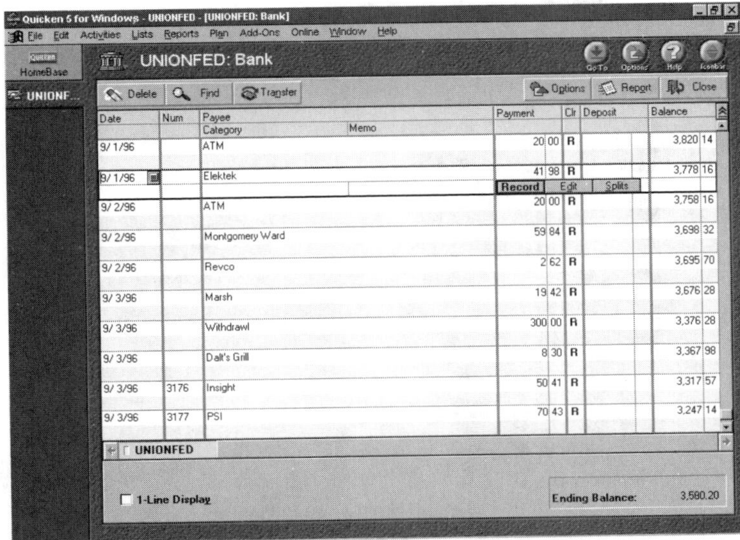

FIGURE 5.19
...or import/export records with Quicken.

QMate is shareware, requiring that you pay $15 to use it beyond a few days.

QuickSheet

QuickSheet, by Cutting Edge Software, is the first and only full-featured spreadsheet for the PalmPilot. Complex calculations can be made quickly and easily with QuickSheet and data can be rapidly analyzed. QuickSheet supports:

- Standard math operators: add (+), subtract (-), multiply (*), divide (/), power (^), and parentheses ()
- Cell formatting includes justification, precision, percent, currency, bold, commas, underline, and more
- Functions SUM, AVG, MIN, MAX, CNT, PMT, IF, NPV, IRR, SQRT, and NOW
- Compatibility with Excel, along with data-transfer capability to/from the desktop
- Linking between sheets
- And many more Excel-like features

QuickSheet is most likely the ultimate tool for financial management due to its ability to construct dynamic, custom financial models and powerful calculations.

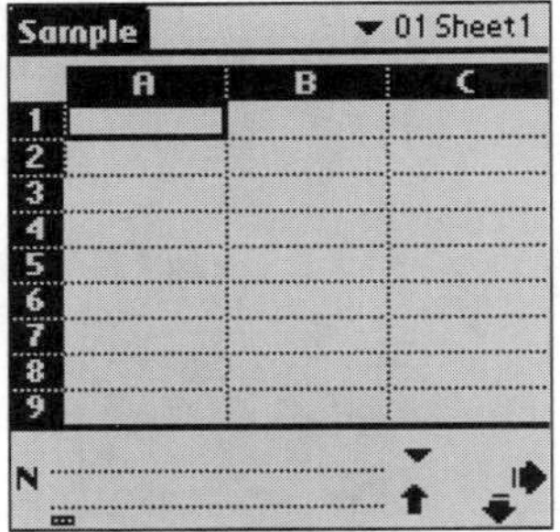

FIGURE 5.20

QuickSheet brings a full-featured spreadsheet to your PalmPilot.

Using QuickSheet, you can build and analyze almost any calculation imaginable. Because it's a spreadsheet, you can dynamically change values to adjust the calculations as necessary. Entering functions can be accomplished by selecting them from a pop-up list or by entering them in Graffiti.

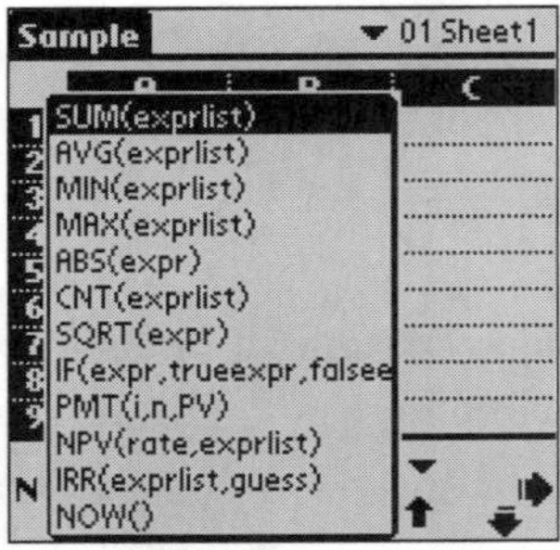

FIGURE 5.21

Enter functions easily by selecting them from a pop-up list.

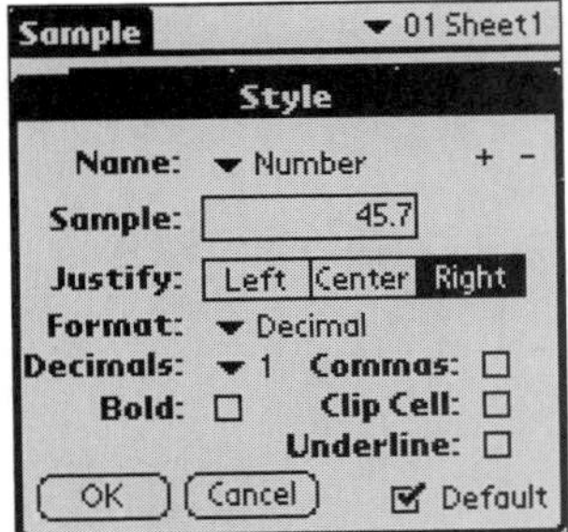

FIGURE 5.22
Cells can be formatted in a variety of ways, using styles or per-cell formatting.

Each individual sheet can be assigned to a category for organizational and sorting purposes. QuickSheet is compatible with Microsoft Excel. Spreadsheets created in QuickSheet can be exported to the desktop and edited in Excel. (At the time of this writing, there is no Mac connectivity support for QuickSheet.)

NOTE QuickSheet's capabilities come in a relatively small package—65K on your PalmPilot. However, QuickSheet requires 200K of free memory for installation. Each spreadsheet you create will take up memory according to its size and complexity, starting at about 4K.

QuickSheet is commercial software that retails for $49.95. Check out Cutting Edge Software's Web site for more information on QuickSheet (**www.cesinc.com**).

CHAPTER 6

Staying Connected

When the Pilot 1000 was first released, it gained critical acclaim for the ease with which it connected to the user's desktop computer. The included cradle and desktop software made data backup and sharing a breeze.

It didn't take long for Pilot 1000 software developers to come up with applications that made use of the Pilot 1000's integrated serial port for more than just desktop connectivity. Third-party conduits and connectivity software for online services are now commonplace in the PalmPilot world.

This chapter will examine the basics behind the PalmPilot's HotSync options and the myriad third-party applications for connecting the PalmPilot to other services.

HotSync Basics

The PalmPilot's HotSync options allow the near-seamless transfer of data between the PalmPilot and the desktop computer. This simple conduit uses the PalmPilot's serial port and a serial port on the desktop computer as the channel for information, but what's behind the scene? This section will show you the "hows and whys" of HotSync on a Windows 95 computer.

HotSync Glossary

Before reading this section, you should understand the terminology related to the PalmPilot, which is set forth in Table 6.1.

Table 6.1 PalmPilot HotSync Glossary

Word/Phrase	Meaning
Conduit	A special piece of software that handles the data transfer for a particular PalmPilot database or module. For example, the addrcond.dll conduit handles the data transfer for the Address Book. Most third-party applications that HotSync their data need their own conduit for dealing with the data.
HotSync	The act of synchronizing the PalmPilot's data with your desktop machine.
Database	A collection of related data on the PalmPilot, generally related by application. For example, all your contacts and their associated data is stored in the Address Book database.
Record	A single element of a database. For example, each name in your Address Book, and its related data, is a record of the Address Book database.
PalmPilot Database	A collection of related information stored on the PalmPilot. On the desktop computer, these files have a PDB (PalmPilot Database) extension. For example, the DinkyPad database is `dinkydat.pdb`. Note that, occasionally, database files are stored with a DAT extension.
PalmPilot Resource	A piece of code or self-contained data used to run the PalmPilot. On the desktop computer, these files have a PRC (PalmPilot Resource) extension. For example, the code for DinkyPad is stored in a file named `dinkypad.prc`.
Windows Registry	A file in which Windows 95 stores configuration information for itself and practically all of its applications. The PalmPilot Desktop and HotSync Manager store their settings in this file.

HotSync Manager

The basic brains behind the HotSync operation is the HotSync Manager. This small application usually runs minimized within Windows 95 until the PalmPilot calls for it.

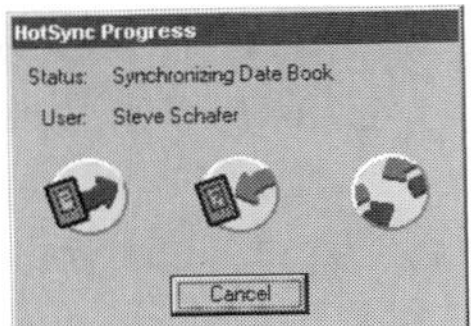

FIGURE 6.1
HotSync Manager is the brains behind the synchronization of the PalmPilot's data with the desktop.

The HotSync Manager decides what data needs to be transferred to and from the PalmPilot and manages the actual communication in and out of the desktop computer's serial port.

NOTE There are other alternatives to running HotSync Manager besides having it minimized on the desktop. By choosing Hide from the Options menu of HotSync, Manager 1.1 will cause it to go into hiding, disappearing from the desktop entirely. Run HotSync Manager again to restore it to the desktop. (Windows will make the window visible again instead of running another copy.) You might also consider only running the HotSync Manager when you need it. However, this can significantly decrease the usefulness of HotSyncing, removing the "anytime, on demand" appeal.

HotSync Manager 2.x runs in the Tray of Windows 95, where it is practically invisible anyway. This version also includes an "Available only when PalmPilotDesktop is running" option from its Setup menu. This option will run the HotSync Manager when you start up the PalmPilotDesktop and will exit the manager when you exit the desktop.

The HotSync Manager takes its data cues from information stored in the Windows Registry. This information tells the manager how to synchronize each module of the PalmPilot by specifying the default conduit and synchronization options. For example, the HotSync Manger typically uses the `addcond.dll` conduit for data transfer to and from the Address Book and normally does a full synchronization, updating PalmPilot and desktop with changes from each other.

The PalmPilot creates an *identifier* for each record it stores in each database. This identifier is used to keep track of records and changes within records for the HotSync Manager. For example, if you change the home telephone number of a person in your Address Book, that number will be changed in the record on the desktop next time you HotSync. If the manager encounters conflicting data, it simply duplicates the conflicting record. For example, if you change a home number on the desktop and PalmPilot (and they don't match), you will have two records (one for each change) after your next HotSync. In reality, the PalmPilot is perceiving two different records because the identifiers it creates for the two records are different.

TIP Duplicate records are bad—avoid them at all costs. It is difficult to recover from duplicates and they tend to multiply as you try to sort them out. To help avoid duplicate records, only change data on the desktop or the PalmPilot (not both!) between HotSyncs.

The HotSync Manager stores data in a folder with the user's ID. For example, my data is stored in a `SchafeS` folder in my PalmPilot directory because my user ID is "Steve Schafer." The manager assumes your ID is a name and uses up to the first seven characters of the second word (last name) and the first letter of the first word (first name). Each individual database has its own folder under the user ID folder where data from the PC—destination PalmPilot—is stored. For example, my PalmPilot folder resembles:

```
PalmPilot
      SchafeS
            address
            Backup
            CASL
            datebook
            expense
            Install
            Mail
            memopad
            QMate
            todo
```

NOTE This folder is for a PalmPilot Pro with Qmate, the CASL runtime module, and Mail installed.

Each user has his/her own data folder in the PalmPilot folder, making it possible for multiple users to share the same cradle on the same desktop computer. When using the PalmPilot Desktop software, you must select the appropriate user ID if you are using a shared cradle.

> **CAUTION** Be careful not to give two PalmPilots the same name—otherwise, you risk confusing HotSync Manager and possible data loss!

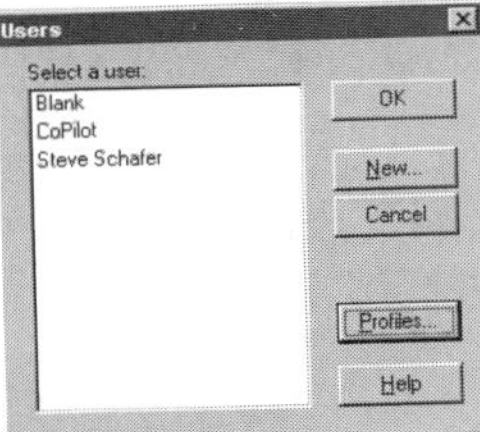

FIGURE 6.2
If the HotSync Manager doesn't recognize the PalmPilot, you need to select a profile or create a new one.

> **TIP** Check out the Help Notes on the official PalmPilot Web page for helpful information about avoiding and preventing HotSync problems. You can find Help Notes at **www.usr.com/palm/custsupp**.

Installing Software

The HotSync Manager also installs any new software on your PalmPilot. To install new software, you must use the Install Application program (instapp) that comes with the PalmPilot software. This application takes the name of a database or resource file and makes the necessary arrangements for the manager to install it. Specifically, Install Application does the following two things:

- Copies the file specified to the appropriate Install folder (\Pilot*userID*\Install).
- Marks the appropriate entry in the Windows Registry for "Install," so the manager knows it needs to install the files.

NOTE Remember to set the correct User Name on the Install Application program if you are using multiple PalmPilots with one desktop computer.

▶ **See** For more information on installing software in your PalmPilot, check out your PalmPilot manual, Chapter 11, "Installing Applications on your PalmPilot."

Use of the Install Application program is straightforward; simply run the program and specify the file to be installed. If you know the full path and file name of the program to install, enter it in the File Name field. If necessary, you can use the Browse button to find the file. After making arrangements for the file, Install Application will ask if you want to install another application. This makes it easy to install multiple applications at once.

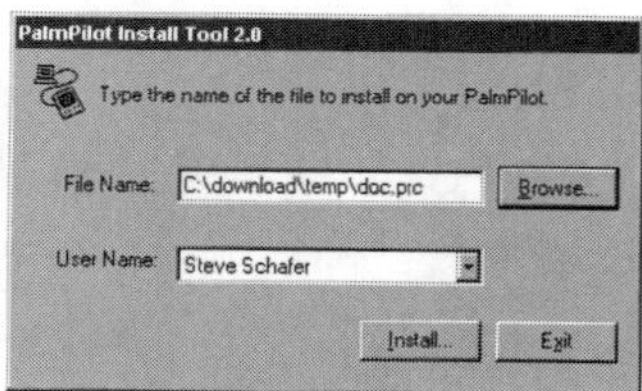

FIGURE 6.3
The Install Application is easy to use–simply point it at the application you want to install and make sure the correct profile is selected.

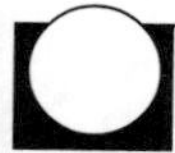

TIP Create a shortcut to the Install Application and place it on your desktop. Then, drag files out of the Finder or Explorer onto the shortcut to quickly install them. Also, if you associate PRC files with INSTAPP, you can simply double-click the PRC file to bring up the Install Application program.

Alternatively, check out Eric Eilebrecht's *Silent App Installer* (SAP). This little program simply sets the specified file for installation–no dialogs, no waiting. Download SAP and associate your PRC files with it for quick and painless installations.

Inside the Registry

The Windows 95 Registry is used to store a log of information about the PalmPilot Desktop, installed conduits, and HotSync options. Specifically, the following data is tracked in the Registry:

- The path of the default PalmPilot folder.
- The path to the HotSync Manager.
- The name of any data to install and a unique key pointing to the name of the PalmPilot on which the application should be installed.
- HotSync Manager settings (COM port, ask on exit, and so on).
- Conduit information on each application or component.

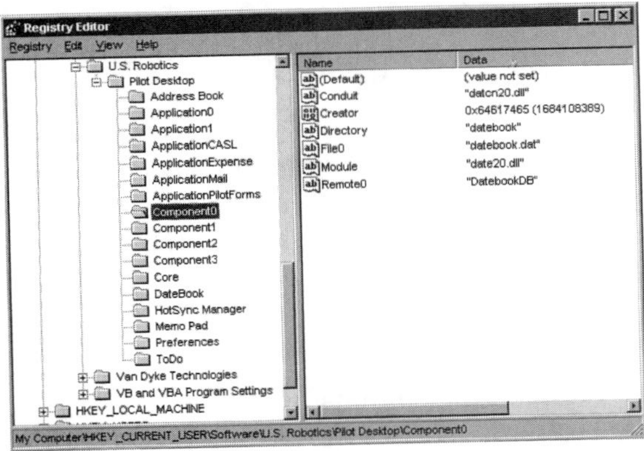

FIGURE 6.4

The Windows 95 Registry contains a lot of information about the PalmPilot Desktop and the PalmPilot itself.

Version 1.x of the PalmPilot Desktop stores its settings in the Registry under `HKEY_CURRENT_USER\Software\Palm Computing\Pilot Desktop`. PalmPilot Desktop version 2.x stores its setting under `HKEY_CURRENT_USER\Software\US Robotics\Pilot Desktop`. You can use RegEdit to view the various settings in the Registry.

Windows 3.1 users can find settings in the `pilot.ini` file in their Windows directory, with similar settings to those mentioned here. Use Notepad or your favorite text editor to view this file.

CAUTION Resist the urge to tinker with the configuration parameters in the Registry by using the RegEdit program. Not only can this interfere with future HotSyncs, but it also could result in lost data!

TIP If you have installed and removed one of the mail applications that uses Memo Pad, you might find that you can no longer synchronize your memos. If you experience this problem, look for an ApplicationX entry in the Registry under the PalmPilot Desktop settings ("X" will be a single digit number), where the "Remote0" entry is "memoDB," but the Conduit is not "memcnXX." ("XX" will be the OS version you are using.) Deleting this entry should restore Memo Pad synchronization.

Synchronizing with Multiple Desktop Machines

It is possible to synchronize your PalmPilot with multiple desktop computers, such as your office and home machines. To avoid data problems, follow this simple rule:

> Don't do it.

However, if you find that you simply must synchronize your PalmPilot at two separate locations, avoid editing or adding information on both desktops. Doing so can cause duplicate records or discrepancies in your PalmPilot's data.

TIP 3Com Corporation has a Help Note for users who synchronize with several desktop systems. Check out the official PalmPilot Web page at **www.usr.com/palm/custsupp** for more details.

Modem HotSync

The PalmPilot also has the ability to HotSync remotely by using a modem. The HotSync Manager must be set in "modem" mode on a computer with a modem attached. The remote PalmPilot user simply follows these steps:

1. Connect the PalmPilot to a modem using the cradle or the special PalmPilot serial cable.
2. Run the HotSync application.

3. Enter the telephone number of the remote system running the HotSync Manager.
4. Select "Modem Sync" to let the PalmPilot dial and synchronize with the remote system.

NOTE The PalmPilot supports a limited number of modem types. Before attempting a remote modem HotSync, check out the Modem Setup options in the HotSync application on your PalmPilot.

This feature can be invaluable for companies who have remote employees with PalmPilots. Using the modem feature, these employees can synchronize their data with the home office, who can then archive or use the information sent to the local desktop. For example, if an outside sales force uses PalmPilots, their customer lists and orders can be sent to the home office via HotSync.

TIP U.S. Robotics released the PalmPilotModem, a small, self-contained 14,400 fax/modem that attaches to your PalmPilot. The PalmPilotModem can be used with any application that requires a modem and it fits nicely in your pocket. Find the modem at local retailers or through 3Com Corporation for around $125 retail.

Network HotSync

At the time of this writing, 3Com Corporation is working on software that will allow PalmPilot Pro users to HotSync across a local area network. The software is slated to be available in June, 1997, and to retail for around $70. Network HotSync will only work with Windows 95 or NT running TCP/IP.

Check the official PalmPilot Web site (**www.usr.com/palm/**) for more information.

NOTE Only the PalmPilot Pro (or 2.0 upgrades with 1M memory) will have the capability to HotSync over a network because it is the only PalmPilot model that has TCP/IP connectivity

Backing Up Your Data

There are times when HotSyncing your data isn't enough when you need bulletproof data backup for your PalmPilot. That's where

Ripcord, by Harry Ohlsen of Industrial Software Engineering, comes in handy.

Ripcord is an application specifically designed to install multiple applications onto your PalmPilot and to back up the data currently on it. This function is particularly important for solving memory fragmentation problems or recovering from a hard reset.

Full use of Ripcord requires a lot of faith in the program because you have to start with a full HotSync, then a hard reset, which loses all the data on your PalmPilot. You then use Ripcord to reinstall all of your applications from the PalmPilot's Backup directory. As it installs the software, Ripcord builds an inventory of the installed applications and optimizes the memory they occupy.

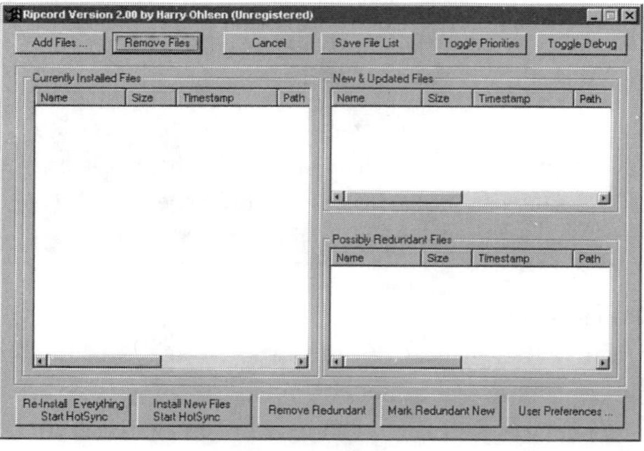

FIGURE 6.5
Ripcord helps you organize your PalmPilot data and provides a full backup and restore if necessary.

TIP It is highly recommended that you read the documentation and caveats supplied with Ripcord before attempting to use it. Failure to do so might result in significant data loss!

Connecting with Other Organizers

There are many Organizer and Personal Information Manager products for desktop computers. If you are like me, you have been using one or more of these products far longer than you have been using your PalmPilot and you aren't inclined to give it up anytime soon.

Or, perhaps you need more functionality on your desktop than the PalmPilot Desktop can provide. Luckily, there are several solutions available to connect your PalmPilot to your favorite desktop schedule, organizer, or PIM program.

TIP There are several solutions for synchronizing your PalmPilot with most desktop applications; some applications have PalmPilot connectivity built in. When in doubt, contact your Organizer or PIM manufacturer and ask what connectivity software they recommend or support for use with the PalmPilot. Be sure to verify that their solution works with the version of HotSync and PalmPilot OS that you currently have.

Intellisync

Intellisync, by Puma Technology, was one of the premier synchronization programs, supporting the following applications:

- Outlook 97
- Lotus Organizer 97
- NetManage ECCO 4.0
- GoldMine 3.0, 3.2
- Internet Sidekick
- Lotus Organizer 2.1
- Microsoft Schedule+ for Windows 95 7.0 and 7.0a
- Sidekick for Windows 1.0, 2.0, and Windows 95
- Now Up-to-Date for Windows and Windows 95
- DayTimer Organizer 2.0, 2.1

Intellisync offers one-button synchronization to these applications, transferring most data to or from the desktop. It offers conflict resolution, sorting out data problems on its own without your intervention.

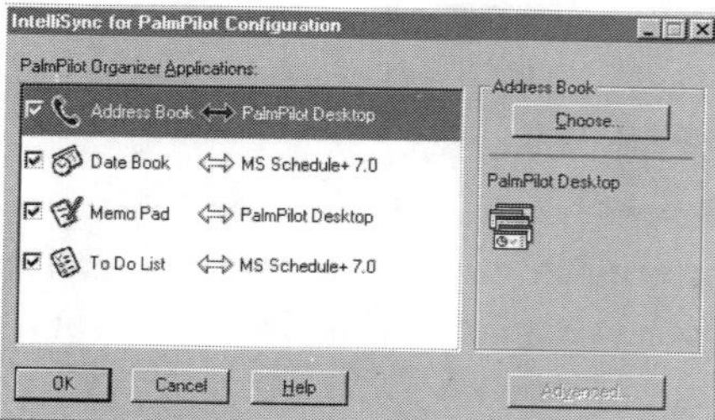

FIGURE 6.6
Intellisync provides PalmPilot connectivity to MS Schedule+ as well as several other applications.

PilotMirror

PilotMirror, by Chapura, allows you to synchronize your PalmPilot's Date Book, Address Book, To Do List, and Memo Pad with Outlook 97's Calendar, Contacts, Tasks, and Notes folders.

PilotMirror is relatively new in the market, but initial reviews are quite positive. If you are using Outlook, you might want to check out Chapura's Web page for more information (**www.chapura.com**).

Integral PalmPilot Support

Some Organizer and PIM software comes complete with support for the PalmPilot. For example:

- Franklin Quest has a package complete with a PalmPilot and a special version of Agenda that links with the PalmPilot.
- NetManage's Ecco has had PalmPilot synchronization for the last several versions—with version 4.01, the connectivity is practically seamless.
- Lotus Development Corp. has announced plans to develop connectivity between the PalmPilot and their applications.
- Symantec is building connectivity for ACT! users.
- Starfish Software has connectivity in the works for Sidekick 97.

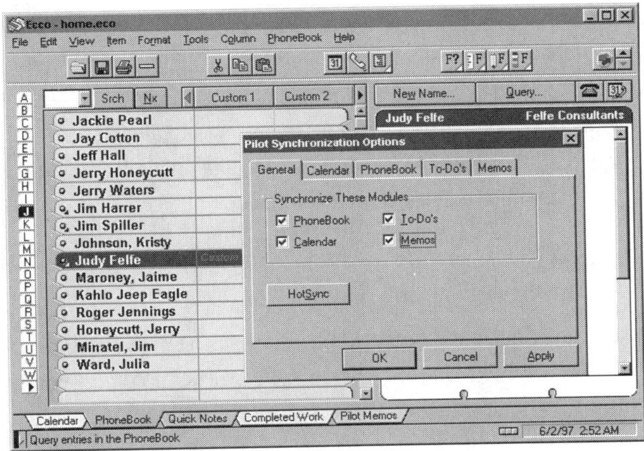

FIGURE 6.7
You can select what to synchronize on the next HotSync by using menus found inside Ecco.

Call your software's manufacturer to find out if they support the PalmPilot or have plans to in the near future.

E-Mail Connectivity

Consider this: You have to leave on a business trip within the hour but have a backlog of e-mail on your computer. Or, suppose you are on the trip but remember some important data a client was going to e-mail to you. On a more personal side, what if you want to e-mail to your sister a friend's contact information, which is stored on your PalmPilot?

Each of these problems has a common solution—e-mail for the PalmPilot. HotSync your e-mail to your PalmPilot and take it with you on the trip, use a modem to HotSync from a remote location and retrieve that valuable e-mail, or cut and paste the contact information into a message and send it to your sister.

The capability to travel with e-mail on the PalmPilot was high on the list of "must haves" from the PalmPilot-using community. To that end, Mail connectivity was added to the PalmPilot Pro, and several third-party vendors have developed e-mail applications. Some of those applications are described in later sections of this chapter.

NOTE This list of PalmPilot e-mail applications is not complete. There are several other e-mail clients available for the PalmPilot, with more showing up all the time. The e-mail applications presented here are the most popular, as demonstrated by messages on the PalmPilot newsgroups and mail lists. Check out your favorite online PalmPilot source for more information about PalmPilot e-mail.

PalmPilotMail

The PalmPilot Pro (and Pilot 1000/5000 Pro upgrade) provides the ability to connect with your desktop computer's e-mail client. Using a new Mail application and conduit, PalmPilot Pro can read and send mail from the following e-mail applications:

- Microsoft Outlook 97
- Microsoft Exchange 4.0
- Windows for Workgroups Mail
- Lotus cc:Mail (version 2.5, 6, or 7)

NOTE Any Simple MAPI or VIM e-mail client may be compatible with PalmPilotMail. If your client uses MAPI, try selecting Exchange in the HotSync Manager configuration. If your client uses VIM, select CCI:Mail 2.5. Check the official Pilot Web page for more information on unsupported e-mail clients.

PalmPilotMail is the most capable e-mail package for the PalmPilot, but requires that you have a working, compatible desktop e-mail client.

To set up PalmPilotMail for use with your desktop mail system, choose Custom from the HotSync Manager's menu, select Mail from the application list, and click the Change button. Next, check the "Activate PalmPilotMail" check box, select your e-mail program, fill out the relevant fields, and then click OK.

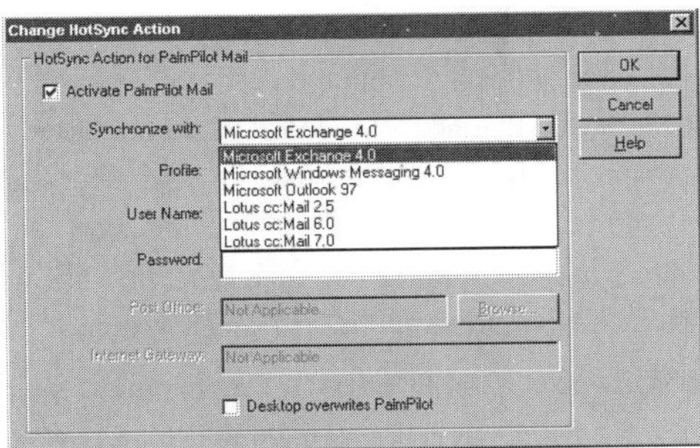

FIGURE 6.8
PalmPilotMail connects to most MAPI- and VIM-compliant mail applications, including MS Exchange.

Note that the PalmPilotMail application requires HotSync to receive or send mail and that your desktop e-mail client is actually used to read and send the mail. Also note that PalmPilotMail supports only text messaging and has a limit of 8,000 characters per message.

To receive messages on your PalmPilot, make sure your desktop e-mail client is running and then perform a HotSync. The HotSync Manager will log into your mail system and synchronize your mail according to the setting in the Manager and PalmPilotMail. After the HotSync, you can access the PalmPilotMail program and read your messages from the Inbox.

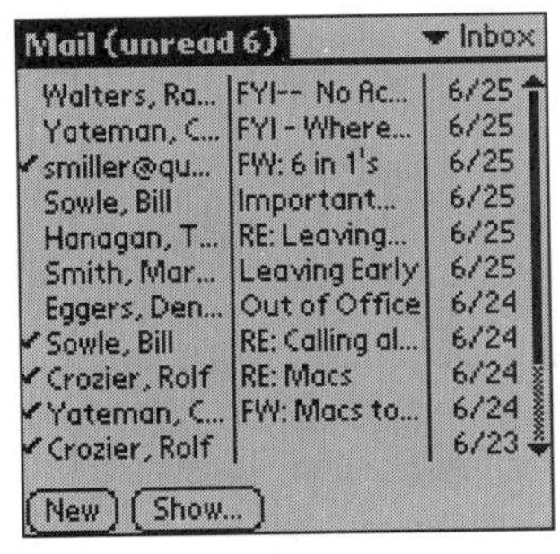

FIGURE 6.9
Messages are transferred to your PalmPilot by using the rules you have specified.

NOTE Occasionally, when HotSyncing large amounts of data, the PalmPilot seemingly will lose connection with the desktop computer. What generally happens is that the PalmPilot doesn't receive data from the desktop for a certain amount of time (because the desktop is busy assembling the data) and the PalmPilot assumes the connection has been lost. This is prone to happen in Mail due to the time the HotSync Manager must spend retrieving data from the Host's mail system.

If this problem persists, try setting the PalmPilot in "Wait Forever" mode. This mode was put into the PalmPilot for developers to use for testing and troubleshooting, but can be activated for your use. To activate this mode, follow these steps:

1. Access the HotSync application on the PalmPilot.
2. Hold both the up and down scroll buttons and tap the upper-right corner of the screen.
3. A window will pop-up titled "DEVELOPER'S BACKDOOR" with the text: "

   "DLServer Wait Forever is ON."
4. Tap OK.
5. Now perform the HotSync again.

The "Wait Forever" mode will be active only until the completion of the next HotSync or until the PalmPilot powers itself off. Use this mode whenever necessary to complete a large HotSync.

Writing new mail messages is straightforward. Simply tap the New button on the main screen of PalmPilotMail and enter the address to which you want to send the message, the subject, and the message. You can also enter an address to receive a copy of the message (CCl, or carbon copy) if you want.

TIP You can use the Lookup feature to quickly enter a recipient's e-mail address. If the recipient is in your Address Book and has their e-mail address included, you can enter that address by specifying the first few characters of their name in the To or CC field and choosing Lookup from the Mail application's Options menu. If the PalmPilot is able to find an Address Book entry based on the characters you entered, that e-mail address will be entered in the appropriate field. If the PalmPilot cannot identify a unique record, it will display your Address Book and allow you to choose the appropriate record. (Use Lookup on a blank field to display the list by default.)

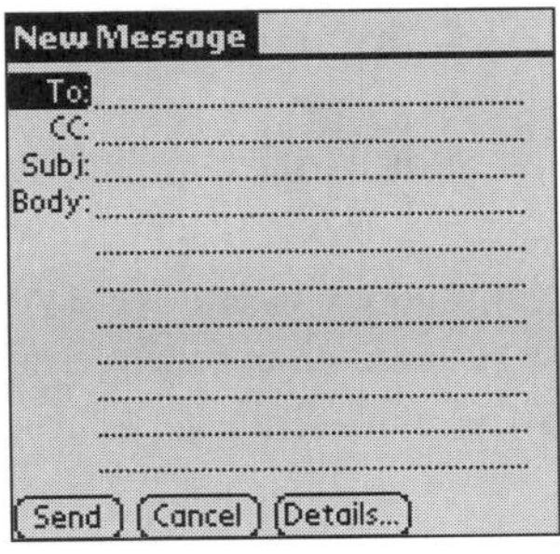

FIGURE 6.10
Entering a new message in PalmPilotMail is easy—and it synchronizes to your desktop e-mail program with the next HotSync.

You can specify additional delivery information by using the Details button while composing a new message. Using these "details," you can specify the priority of the message, request that the CCl be blind (BCCl), add your electronic signature (defined in the Preferences of Mail) to the end of the message, and ask for receipts when the mail is read or delivered.

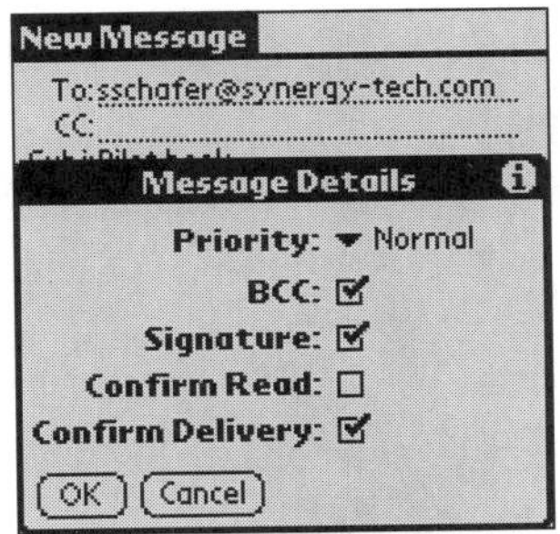

FIGURE 6.11
PalmPilotMail delivery options provide BCCl, signature, and receipt options.

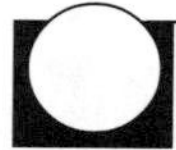

TIP Though some of these Pilot e-mail applications require a desktop e-mail client to function, keep in mind that you can still retrieve your e-mail remotely by using modem HotSync to access the desktop computer.

Palmeta Mail

Palmeta Mail, by Palmeta Software, adds e-mail connectivity to your PalmPilot by adding a new conduit to Memo Pad. This new conduit transfers mail in and out of your Memo Pad, to and from your existing desktop computer's e-mail client. Palmeta uses three new categories in Memo Pad for transferring mail—Inbox, Outbox, and Sent.

After installing Palmeta Mail, you need to use the configuration utility to tell the Palmeta conduit how you want to deal with your mail. You need to tell Palmeta what client e-mail package you use and then decide between several options for sending and receiving messages. After making your selections, the configuration utility will update the Windows Registry with your choices, which will be effective on the next HotSync.

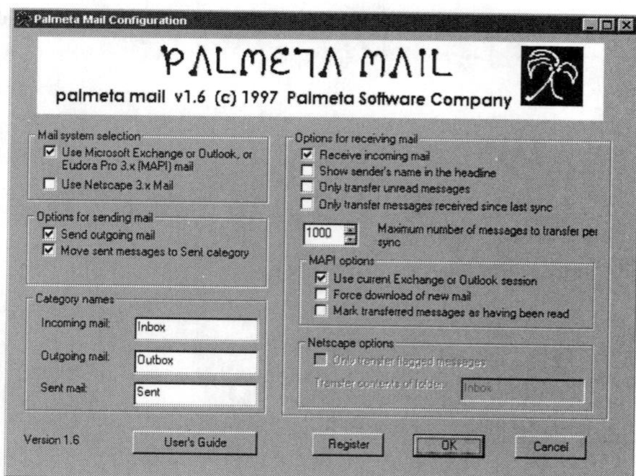

FIGURE 6.12

The Palmeta Configuration utility informs HotSync how to handle your e-mail transfers.

NOTE You need to exit and restart the HotSync Manager for the changes you make with the Palmeta configuration utility to take effect.

The Palmeta conduit retrieves messages from your desktop e-mail client and places them in the Memo Pad as new memos in the Inbox category. Use Memo Pad to read the messages, delete them, and so forth.

To send a message, create a new memo in the Outbox category. The first several lines of the message include the addressing information and the subject of the message. The rest of the memo constitutes the body of the message. The next HotSync will send the messages to the Outbox of your client e-mail program and move the message(s) from the Outbox category to the Sent category.

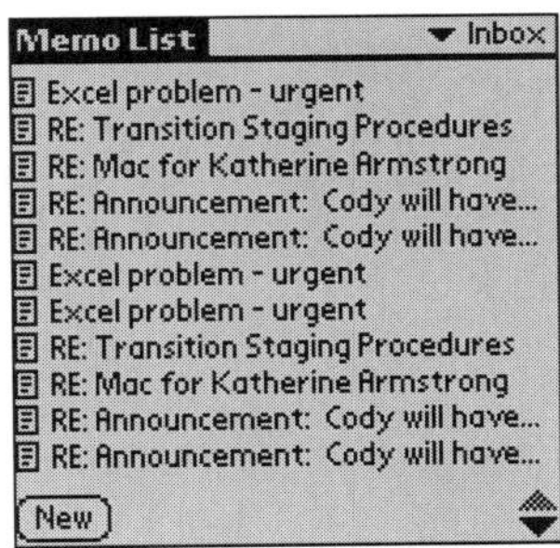

FIGURE 6.13
New messages show up in the Memo Pad's Inbox category.

Like PalmPilotMail, Palmeta Mail requires a client e-mail program on the desktop computer. However, unlike PalmPilotMail, Palmeta Mail will work on any model of PalmPilot, and takes up no valuable RAM space (conduit only).

NOTE Palmeta Mail is shareware—the free copy will send and receive only a limited number of messages. Registration ($39.95) will give you a key to remove this restriction.

StingerMail

StingerMail, by StingerSoft, is an add-on for Palmeta mail that enables you to quickly enter new messages for Palmeta Mail to send. Accessing StingerMail from the application launcher will take you directly to the Inbox category of Memo Pad.

Pressing the New button while in the Outbox category will automatically fill in the "To" and "Subject" field markers for you. Additional buttons in the Outbox allow you to quickly look up addresses for the To, CC, and BCC fields.

If you use Palmeta Mail, StingerMail is a must-have.

TransAOL

TransAOL, by Vincent Debierre, is a PC-based program that allows you to transfer e-mail and stored messages from your America OnLine client to the Memo Pad, and to send Memo Pad messages through AOL e-mail.

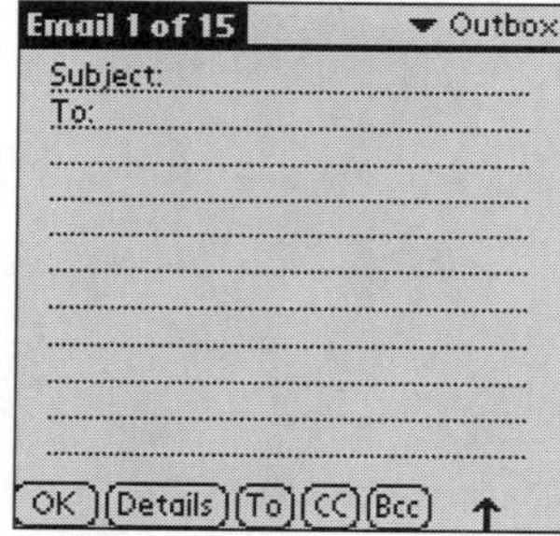

FIGURE 6.14
StingerMail adds true message-composition tools to Palmeta Mail.

TransAOL requires an AOL account and installed AOL software on the desktop computer. TransAOL works much like Palmeta Mail in using Memo Pad categories (Inbox, Outbox, and Sent) for its message management and is StingerMail compatible.

HandStamp

HandStamp, from SmartCode Software, is a full-featured, self-contained Internet e-mail program for the PalmPilot. HandStamp uses its own PPP dialer to connect to the Internet, not needing the TCP/IP connectivity of the PalmPilot to implement the sending and receiving of e-mail across a PPP link.

Unlike the e-mail programs previously discussed, HandStamp does not require a desktop e-mail client and HotSync to function. Instead, HandStamp uses a PPP Internet account and Internet mailbox for its work.

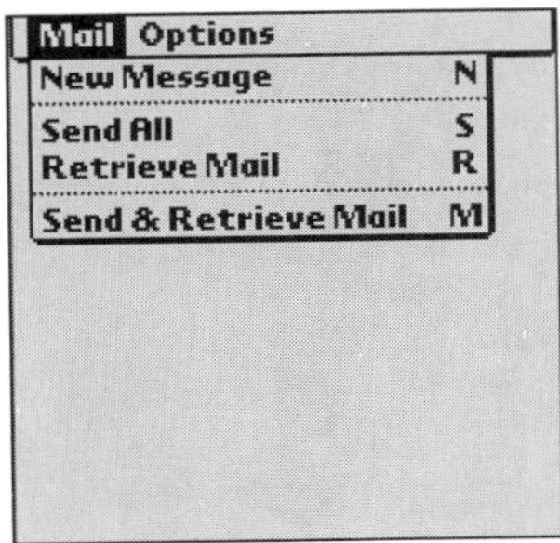

FIGURE 6.15
HandStamp provides full-featured Internet mail connectivity, without the need of a desktop e-mail client.

The set-up of HandStamp is a bit more complex because you have to configure it to dial into your Internet account and access your mailbox. However, once this is complete, using HandStamp is quite effortless.

NOTE HandStamp uses a modem to connect to your Internet mailbox. Therefore, in order to use HandStamp, you must have a dial-in PPP account with an Internet provider and have a modem available for your PalmPilot's use. (The 3Com Corporation PalmPilotModem makes a great traveling companion for your PalmPilot!)

To configure HandStamp, you must set up your modem, which requires knowing your Internet provider's telephone number and the modem commands to initialize your modem. These settings are entered into the Modem Setup screen, accessible from the Modem Setup choice of the HandStamp Options menu.

TIP If you are unsure about what to enter for the Init string of the modem, first try "ATZ." If that does not work, consult your modem manual or Internet provider for additional help.

Secondly, you must set up HandStamp to use your PPP account. This requires your login name, password, and the DNS server IP for your provider. These settings are found under the PPP Setup choice on the Options menu.

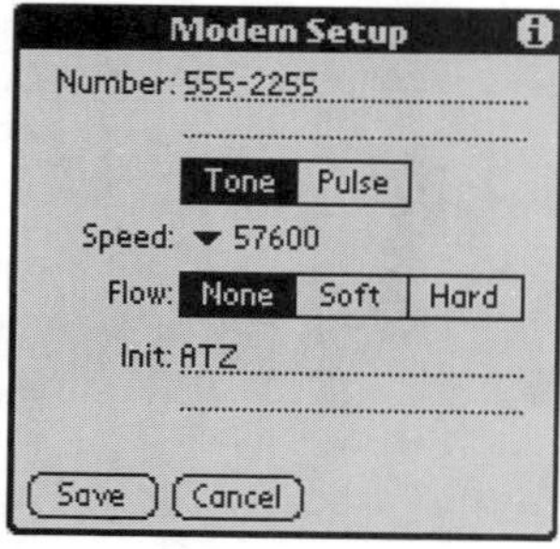

FIGURE 6.16
If you aren't sure what to enter for your modem's Init codes, try "ATZ."

Then, you must tell HandStamp how to log into your provider. A simple script builder is provided in HandStamp under the Connection Script choice of the Options menu. The script builder provides script lines to wait for specific characters, send user-entered characters, send username and password, and to send carriage returns. Use the pull-down menu to select a script command and enter any additional information beside the command.

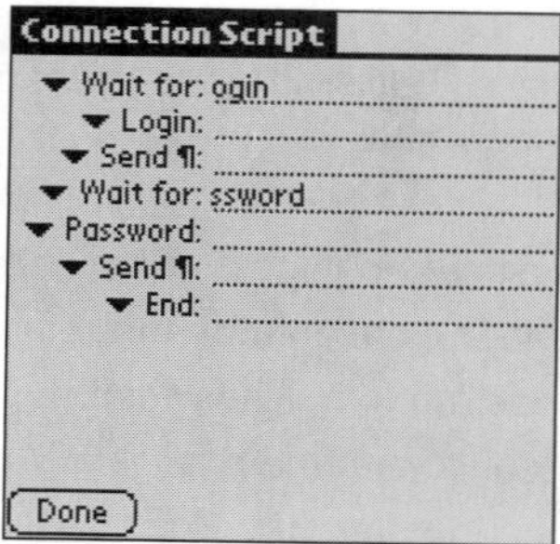

FIGURE 6.17
This script works for most Internet Service Provider's PPP logins.

Lastly, you need to set up your e-mail account information under Mail Preferences in the Options menu. Enter your server and account information, whether you want HandStamp to use Authenticated POP, and whether to leave retrieved mail on the server. Enter your e-mail account information and tap Save to save these preferences.

TIP Generally, it is advantageous to leave the retrieved e-mail on the server until you can retrieve it with an e-mail program that supports attachments and longer files. That way, you won't miss any data that HandStamp can't handle.

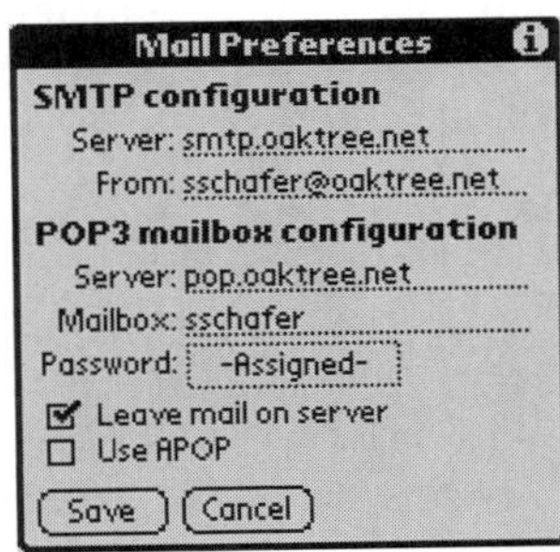

FIGURE 6.18
E-mail preferences are straightforward; just enter your SMTP and POP3 servers and account information.

After finishing the setup, use of HandStamp is similar to desktop-based e-mail clients. To retrieve your mail, select Retrieve Mail from the Mail menu. To send a new message, choose New Message from the Mail menu and then address and compose your message. HandStamp uses its own message editor for reading and composing mail, which can handle messages up to 8,000 characters in length. Messages larger than 8,000 characters will be left on the server.

HandStamp enables you to reply and forward received messages, look up e-mail addresses in the address book, and more. All-in-all, HandStamp is the most full-featured e-mail package available for the PalmPilot.

Simple Terminal and Fax Access

If you are only looking for a way to connect your PalmPilot as a terminal to a remote system, or to send a fax, the following applications will help you:

- *SimpleTerm*, by Iain Barclay, provides simple terminal capability to the PalmPilot's serial port. Using SimpleTerm, you can connect to a remote (text/shell account only) server or bulletin board. To send text, you enter it into a buffer at the bottom of the screen and then tap a Send button. There is a check box that enables an automatic carriage return (enter) after each line.

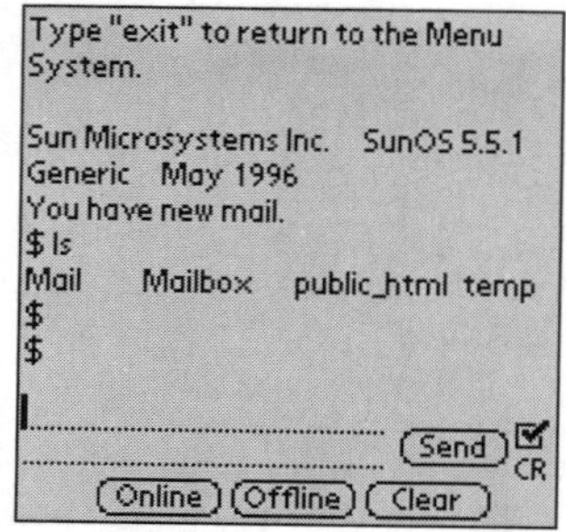

FIGURE 6.19
SimpleTerm provides simple terminal access to online resources.

- *AccessIt!*, by Yamada Tatsushi, is a slightly enhanced version of SimpleTerm, with the same capabilities.

- *Online*, also by Iain Barclay, provides full VT-100 terminal emulation for your PalmPilot. Log onto Unix systems to read mail and even browse the Web (in text mode). Online keeps an 80 × 24 character screen in memory, but due to PalmPilot limitations, it can display only a quarter of the screen at a time. A small navigation tool allows you to quickly scroll around the virtual screen.

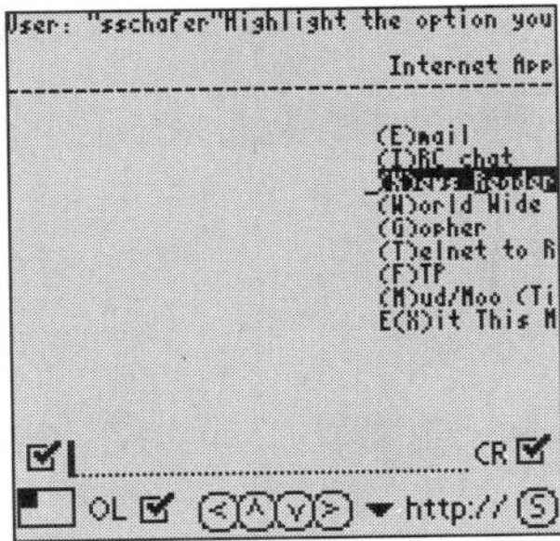

FIGURE 6.20
Full VT-100 support, including arrow keys, allows you to get full use of Unix online resources.

NOTE There are more online utilities popping up all the time, especially now that the PalmPilot Pro includes TCP/IP connectivity. At the time of this writing, there were a few Internet News readers and Web browsers in testing. Check out your favorite online PalmPilot resource for more information.

- *Fax*, by David Bertrand, is a simple application that will use any Class 2 or Class 2.0 fax modem attached to the PalmPilot to send a fax transmission. Fax sends the text stored in the PalmPilot's clipboard or selected Memo Pad document. Fax enables you to customize the page by specifying the fax ID, margins, text size, fax resolution, and a header and footer.

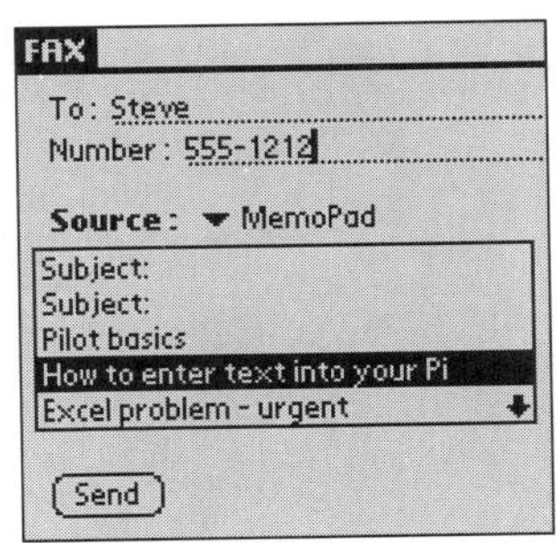

FIGURE 6.21
Place text on the clipboard or select a memo...

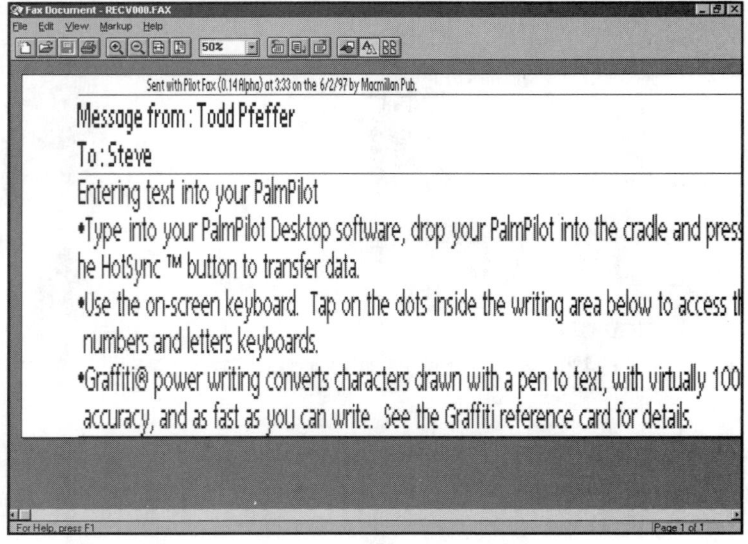

FIGURE 6.22

...and fax it off to someone.

CHAPTER 7

Staying Entertained

Entertainment has always been a driving force in developing programs for any computer hardware platform—and the PalmPilot is no exception. The first third-party games were only a few months behind the Pilot 1000's initial release, scarcely enough time for developers to receive and start using the tools to develop *any* third-party applications!

Today, games remain a popular PalmPilot add-on. To that end, this chapter examines some of the more popular games available.

NOTE This list is far from complete. There are more games than any other category of PalmPilot application; from word guessing and board game adaptations, to arcade games and artificial pets. Check out your favorite online PalmPilot resource for a full list of games for Palm the Pilot.

Space Invaders

One of the very first games for the Pilot 1000 was Scott Ludwig's version of the popular Atari game, Space Invaders. You use a lone planetary gun against a marching horde of alien attackers, racking up points for every alien you shoot down.

Invaders uses the following buttons:

- Date Book — Move left
- Address Book — Move right
- To Do List — Toggle sounds on/off
- Memo Pad — Fire

Using the structures as cover, dodge the alien fire as you pulverize them.

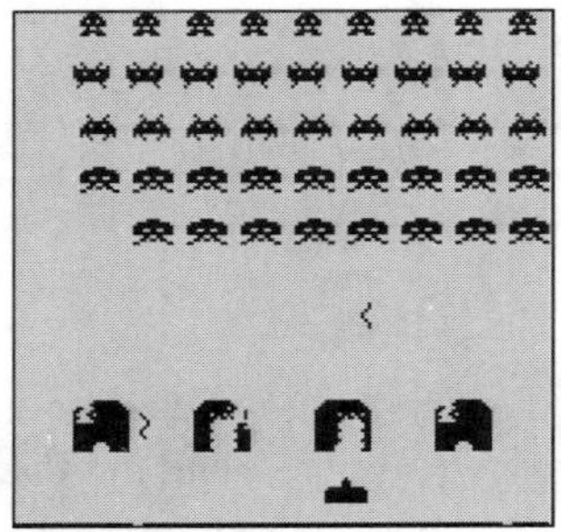

FIGURE 7.1
This brings back memories of the early arcade games!

Reptoids

Reptoids, by Roger Flores, is a close approximation of yet another Atari classic, Asteroids. Piloting a small ship through an asteroid belt, you blast asteroids and alien ships to score points.

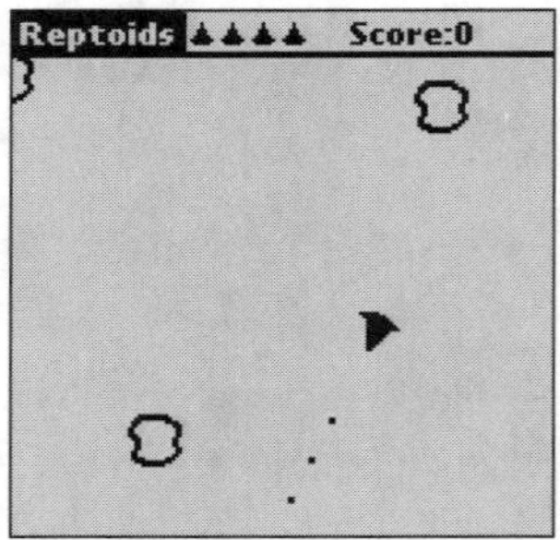

FIGURE 7.2
Asteroids by any other name...

Reptoids uses the following keys:

- Date Book — Turn left
- Address Book — Turn right
- To Do List — Fire
- Memo Pad — Fire thrusters

Missile Command

Another Atari arcade classic has been reborn on the PalmPilot, due to the work of Jesse E. Donaldson. Using on-screen stylus taps, you guide your anti-missile missiles into the air to stop enemy missiles from destroying your cities. With only a limited number of missiles and cities, and the ever-increasing difficulty level, your destruction is imminent—but how high can you score?

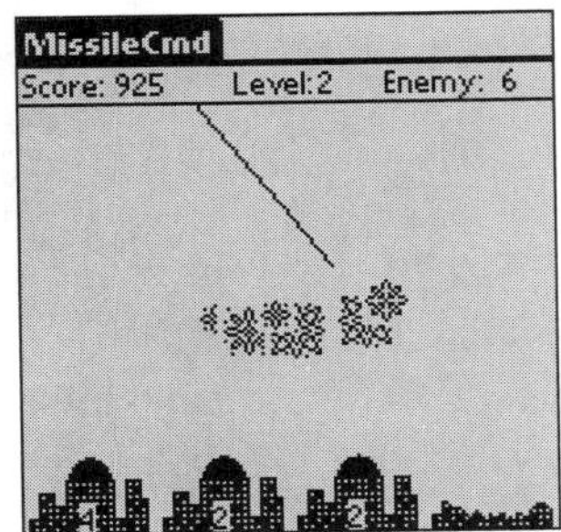

FIGURE 7.3
Another classic, all-time favorite arcade game.

TIP You can pause the game at any time by tapping the Menu button. Continue the game by tapping the button again.

NOTE Another Missile Command game, tentatively titled Defender, is in the works from Tan Kok Mun. However, the PalmPilot public has brought up the fact that there is another arcade game by that name. In any case, look for Tan Kok Mun's version on your favorite online PalmPilot resource.

Pocket Chess

Cool graphics and versions of hit arcade games aside, Scott Ludwig's Pocket Chess is perhaps the most impressive game available for the PalmPilot. Occupying a mere 28K of memory, Pocket Chess provides a full-featured computer chess program. With difficulty settings of 1 through 8, you can pick the level of the computer's proficiency to match your speed.

FIGURE 7.4
Check?!...Again?

Pocket Chess comes complete with options to undo moves, reverse the board, switch sides, show hints for the next move, and options to play against either another human or the PalmPilot. To move pieces, you simply tap the piece you want to move and then tap the square to which you want it to move. Pocket Chess is a must for any PalmPilot enthusiast.

Tricorder

Modeled after the famous scientific instrument in Star Trek, Jeff Jetton's Tricorder provides hours of amusement for the PalmPilot user. Quoting Tricorder's creator: "Sure, the Pilot's great for keeping track of appointments and such, but you can't scan for tachyon emissions with it...until now!"

FIGURE 7.5
Whoa, high Bogon emissions...

Using Tricorder is straightforward for a 24th Century device—simply tap on the controls and push the buttons.

TIP Try using the Bio scan in a Board meeting. Tap the Bio control on the screen and then press one of the scroll buttons.

Wheel Of Fortune

Scott Duensing brings Wheel of Fortune to the PalmPilot. Wheel approximates the real game in every regard, including graphics of Vanna White turning letters, host Pat Sajak, and the infamous letter board. Wheel comes with a puzzle database and instructions for creating your own puzzles for the game.

FIGURE 7.6
Wheel...of...Fortune!

DigiPet

One of the current rages in toyland is the Tamagotchi, or electronic pet. These small devices simulate a pet by demanding attention and food, growing, and eventually dying. Shuji Fukumoto has adapted this concept to the PalmPilot with DigiPet.

DigiPet hatches a pet that you can feed, bathe, scold, pick up after, and play with. When the pet gets lonely, it will demand attention via a PalmPilot alarm. Having rudimentary artificial intelligence, your DigiPet will continue to grow and prosper if you take good care of it. Neglect it and it will die.

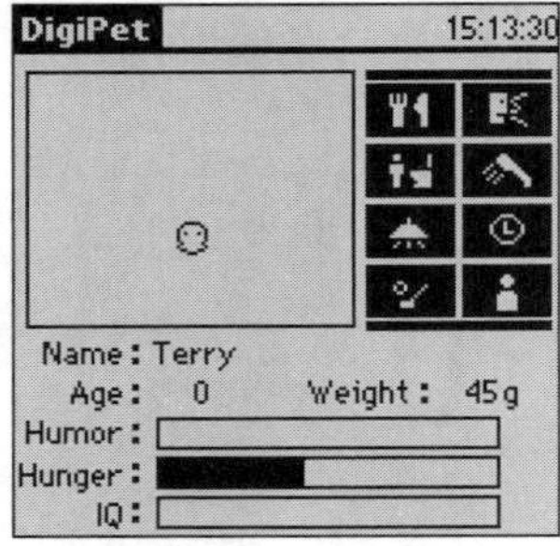

FIGURE 7.7
Take care of your DigiPet or be prepared to bury it.

> **CAUTION** DigiPet will demand attention even if your PalmPilot is off. Be careful not to run DigiPet on low batteries—otherwise, you run the risk of your selfish pet running them dead.

Crossbow

Crossbow, by Harry Ohlsen, is a crossword puzzle program for the PalmPilot. Crossbow uses coded memos stored in a Crossword category for its puzzles. The memos include the puzzle grid and clues for each word. For example, this is part of one of the puzzles that comes with Crossbow:

```
Across
1 Great excitement about black flower (9)
6 Died leading brave retreat in county (5)
9 Rest of old article by novelist (7)
...
Grid
WWWWWWWWWBWWWWW
WBWBWBWBWBWBWBW
WWWWWWWBWWWWWWW
WBWBWBWBWBWBWBW
WWWWWBWWWWWWWWW
WBBBWBWBWBWBWBB
WWWWWWWWBBBWWWW
WBWBWBWBWBWBWBW
WWWWBBBWWWWWWWW
BBWBWBWBWBWBBBW
WWWWWWWWWBWWWWW
WBWBWBWBWBWBWBW
```

```
WWWWWWWBWWWWWWW
WBWBWBWBWBWBWBW
WWWWWBWWWWWWWWW
Down
1 What makes running of course pleasant and relaxed? (4-5)
2 Girl taking in cities in France and America (5)
3 Get very excited about section of contest (8)
...
```

FIGURE 7.8
Solve the puzzles included with Crossbow and then download more or create your own.

To install a new puzzle, you simply cut and paste the puzzle into a Memo in the PalmPilot Desktop and HotSync it to the PalmPilot. To solve a puzzle, you tap a square in a word and then tap "Show Clues" to see the clue for that word.

NOTE There are several additional puzzles online, as well as converters for the *US Today* and *Times* crossword puzzles.

Hangman

A pen-and-paper classic—precursor to the mighty Wheel—makes its way to the PalmPilot. Hangman, by David Haupert, simulates the age-old word guessing game. The shareware/demo copy of Hangman has thirty-five phrases to guess, while the registered version ($12) takes its phrases from a user-customizable database.

FIGURE 7.9
An old pen-and-paper favorite now in digital ink.

Reversi

Reversi, by Julian Jiggins, is a PalmPilot adaptation of a popular strategic board game. The object of the game is to turn as many game pieces to your color as possible. To change a piece's color, you surround it with other pieces of your color.

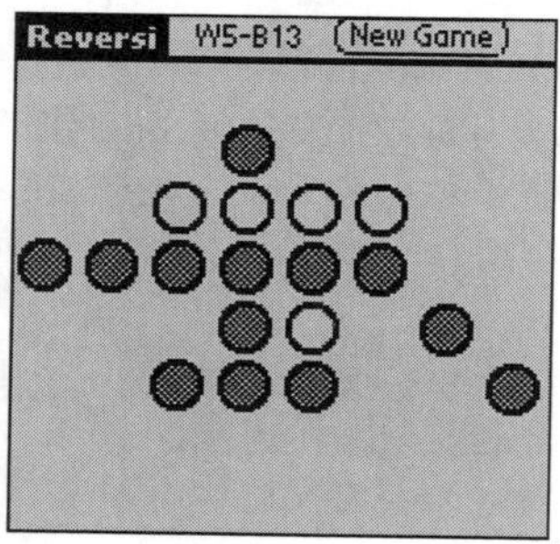

FIGURE 7.10
Another classic board game played against the PalmPilot opponent.

When there are no more spaces to move to, the game is over. The player (human or PalmPilot) who has the most pieces left in play wins.

Black Jack

Stu Slack has brought the game of "21" to the PalmPilot with his Black Jack program. Black Jack allows you to configure the number of decks that are played and supports most known game options (splitting, doubling, etc.).

FIGURE 7.11
Practice before heading to Vegas or Reno!

Black Jack is shareware and will run for 15 days before requiring payment. The registration fee to continue using Black Jack is $14.

PV Poker

PV Poker, by Mike Therien, is a video poker simulator. PV Poker allows bets between 5 and 50 credits, with a starting bank roll of 100 credits and a 5 credit ante.

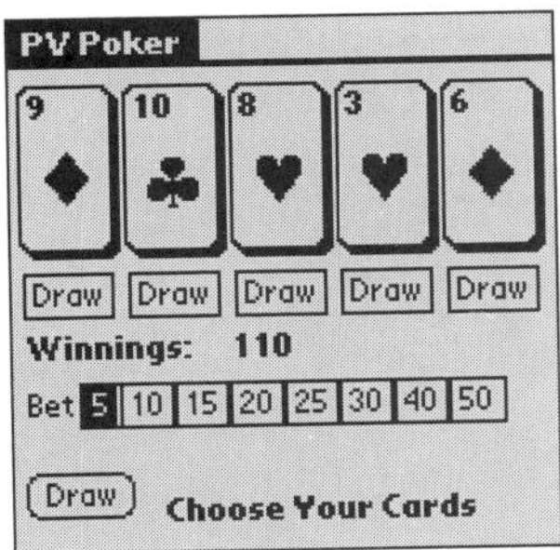

FIGURE 7.12
Got the urge to feed some quarters to a video poker machine? Play on your PalmPilot instead.

FreeCell

Now you can spend as much time procrastinating on your PalmPilot as you do in Windows 95! Bill Kirby's FreeCell plays just like the card game and has several display options for tailoring the display.

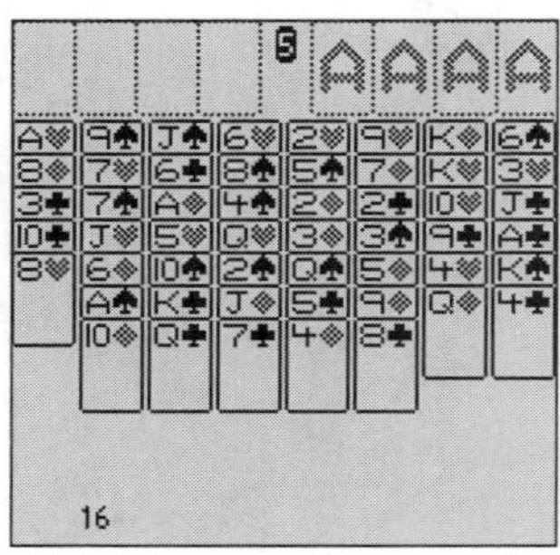

FIGURE 7.13
Tired of solitaire? Try FreeCell.

FreeCell is shareware, allowing you to play for 30 days without registering. Registration for continued use runs $12.

Klondike

Klondike, also by Bill Kirby, is another PalmPilot adaptation of a single-player card game. Like FreeCell, Klondike is shareware, requiring a fee of $12 if used over 30 days.

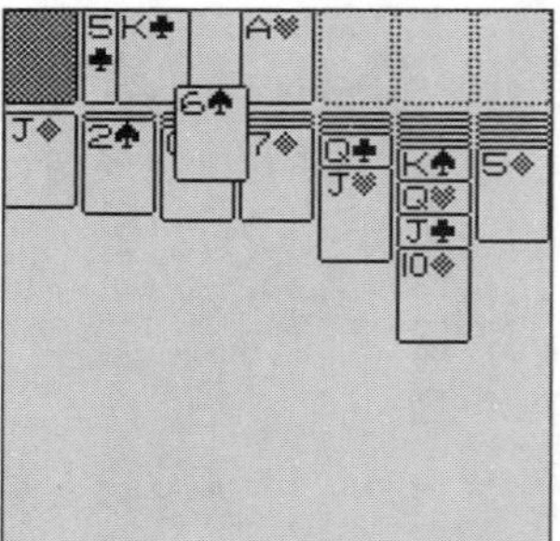

FIGURE 7.14
Another Solitaire-type game for the PalmPilot.

Gem Hunt

Gem Hunt, by Jeff Jetton, is a Mine Hunt-type game. In this version, you fire lasers to get clues as to where the hidden gems are located and then use those clues to uncover the gems.

FIGURE 7.15
Another hidden treasure, numeric clue-type game in the spirit of Mine Hunt.

3Com Corporation Game Pack

Witnessing the popularity of games and entertainment on the PalmPilot, 3Com Corporation has a game pack of its own, including four games of varying types.

MineHunt

Like MineSweeper for Windows, MineHunt is a game of chance and statistical odds. You need to find all the mines in the field without inadvertently uncovering a mine. As you move to safe squares, the squares display numbers, indicating the number of mines that are in the eight squares surrounding that square.

Using the numbers of neighboring squares, you can determine which squares might have mines and avoid them. If you uncover all squares that do not contain mines, you win—uncover a mine and you lose.

FIGURE 7.16
Use the number clues or just blind luck to ferret out the mines.

SubHunt

SubHunt puts you in the captain's seat of a submarine-hunting ship. Using the Date Book and Memo Pad buttons, you move your ship back and forth across the top of the screen. Pressing the Address Book button launches a depth charge from one side of the boat, while pressing the To Do button launches from the other side.

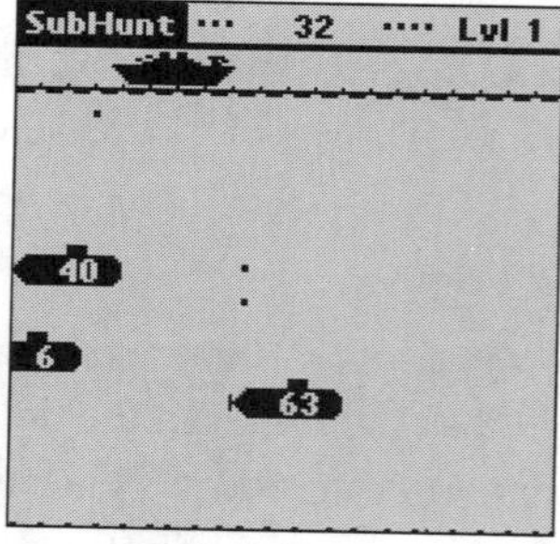

FIGURE 7.17
Use your destroyer to sink the enemy subs before they sink you.

Try to destroy each sub that passes beneath you while avoiding their return fire.

HardBall

Modeled after the arcade game Breakout, HardBall bounces a ball between a paddle and a wall. You control the paddle (and therefore the ball's direction) and each brick disappears as it is hit. You score points for every brick hit and you have a limited number of balls with which to play.

FIGURE 7.18
The old game of Breakout, given new PalmPilot-life.

Puzzle

The old sliding number puzzle rounds out 3Com Corporation's game pack. Slide the numbers around the puzzle and try to get them back in order.

FIGURE 7.19
Slide the numbers back into order.

CHAPTER 8

System Enhancements

Nothing is perfect, that includes the 3Com Corporation PalmPilot. The PalmPilot was engineered to be easy to use and to increase your productivity. 3Com Corporation's new PalmPilot design reflects over a year of customer feedback, bringing many new innovations to the PalmPilot.

However, no matter how well the PalmPilot performs, there are always improvements that can be made, whether to solve software problems or to make the PalmPilot more useful to you.

This chapter will cover the various enhancements to the PalmPilot, from a utility to redefine the PalmPilot's buttons, to a new Operating System.

PalmPilot and Operating System 2.x

The new PalmPilot and its new Operating System (OS), 2.0, incorporates the following features:

- Auto caps—automatically shifts the next character after a punctuation mark to a capital letter.
- Time display—Tap the date in the Date Book to see the current time.
- Busy Bars—Bars in the Date book show the length of each appointment.
- Status Icons—More icons next to appointments show the presence of alarms and notes; tapping these icons lets you edit the property they represent.

- Week Scroll Arrows—Arrows next to the days at the top of the Date Book enable you to quickly scroll between weeks.
- Week View Drag-and-Drop—Appointments can be dragged from their set location and dropped to a new date/time.
- Scroll bars—scroll bars next to long listings can be used to traverse the listings instead of using the scroll buttons.

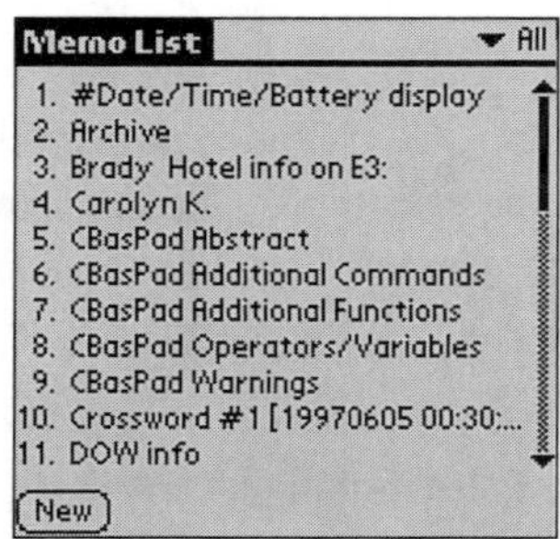

FIGURE 8.1
For easy scrolling, the latest OS adds graphical scroll bars to lists.

- More Intuitive Interface—New interfaces on features like Shortcuts allow for easier and quicker data entry and customization.
- Phone Lookup—PalmPilot applications can automatically insert an Address Book entry by looking up a fragment of a name.
- More Display and Sort Options—The To Do List provides more ways to sort your To Do items and allows more data for each item to be shown.
- Owner Information—A special preferences screen enables the user to enter pertinent data about him/herself, allowing a lost PalmPilot to be returned.
- Expense Manager—A new application enables you to track expenses and HotSync the data to the desktop.
- TCP/IP and E-Mail—The PalmPilot Pro includes TCP/IP connectivity and an e-mail application.

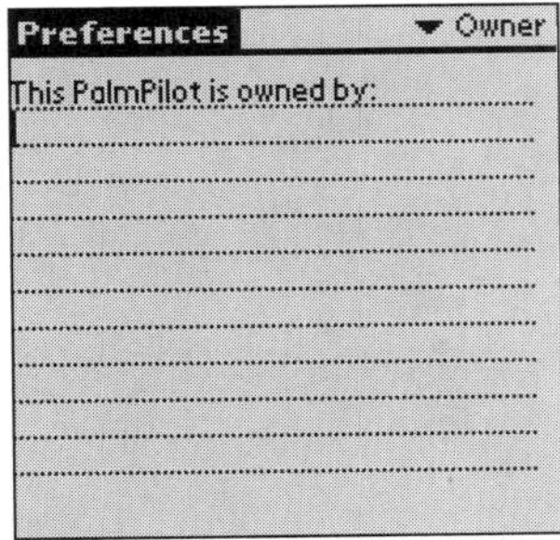

FIGURE 8.2
Enter your contact information so if you lose your PalmPilot, it can be sent back to you.

- Modem Configuration—Several options have been added to control how the PalmPilot talks to a modem through its serial port.
- Conduit Setup—The PalmPilot can now control which conduits are run during a HotSync, which is perfect for remote synchronization.

FIGURE 8.3
Conduits can now be controlled from the PalmPilot instead of just the PalmPilot desktop

NOTE At the time of this writing, 3Com Corporation was offering an upgrade package for Pilot 1000 and 5000 owners. For about $120 (retail), these users can upgrade their Pilot 1000 or 5000 to a 1M PalmPilot Pro with OS 2.x. This upgrade gives the Pilot 1000 and 5000 the same capabilities of the PalmPilot Pro, except for the backlit display.

PalmPilot Upgrades

There have been several upgrades to the PalmPilot since its inception. These upgrades are detailed in this section.

Upgrades to OS 1.x

There were three public upgrades to the original (1.0) Pilot 1000 Operating System, as detailed in the following sections.

Update 1.0.2 The Pilot 1000 and 5000 were shipped primarily with this OS. However, performing a hard reset on the Pilot 1000/5000 will revert back to the ROM version of the OS (1.0). All Pilot 1000/5000 users should have this update handy to recover the OS if a hard reset is ever necessary.

Update 1.0.4 The update to 1.0.4 fixed two problems with earlier operating systems; Pilot 1000s or 5000s who exhibit either of the following two behaviors should upgrade to 1.0.4:

- Pressing an application button while the Pilot 1000 and 5000 is off brings up the previously running application instead of the application defined to the button. Pressing the same application button again brings up the correct application.
- The HotSync button on the cradle requires two presses to activate HotSync. The first press turns on the Pilot 1000 and 5000, but HotSync does not start.

Update 1.0.6 This update to the original OS enhanced the memory allocation and management functions of the Pilot 1000 and 5000. These enhancements result in less memory fragmentation and better overall utilization of memory during application installation.

Upgrades to OS 2.x

There has been only one upgrade to PalmPilot OS 2.0. Update 2.0.1 changes the digitizer sensitivity to help overcome the infamous "Tap Bug."

After the PalmPilot models were released, developers started noticing a bug in the Graffiti pad and PalmPilot screen. This bug caused some random taps to happen on the screen when the user tapped on the left side of the screen. The update eliminates that problem.

HotSync Versions

There have been three versions of HotSync as of the time of this writing:

- HotSync 1.0—Shipped with the original Pilot 1000 and 5000.
- HotSync 1.1—Upgrade to fix a few problems found in version 1.0, such as backing up data for the first 12 applications *only*. This version of HotSync was the first to be adopted by many third-party developers for their custom conduits.
- HotSync 2.0—Fixes the backup problem of version 1.1 where subsequent HotSyncs would not refresh the backup of the PalmPilot's data. HotSync 2.0 works with all models of the PalmPilot family and all versions of the OS. Check for compatibility with HotSync 2.0 if you use any third-party conduits, or synchronize with a third-party scheduler or PIM. As of this writing, most third-party utilities still only support version 1.1.

TIP If you continue to use HotSync version 1.1, move the contents of the Backup directory before performing a HotSync to force HotSync to back up the PalmPilot's data.

Miscellaneous Upgrades

There has been only one other upgrade of note to the PalmPilot—*SlimCalc*. The original PalmPilot 1000 calculator (OS 1.0.2) had a bug that resulted in some erroneous calculations. U.S. Robotics quickly released a calculator upgrade that solved these problems. If you are still using OS 1.x, check your calculator to make sure it is the upgraded version. If the calculator's "+" key is longer than it is wide, then you are running the upgrade. The PalmPilots come with the upgraded calculator.

NOTE The Calculator upgrade is placed in RAM instead of ROM, where the original Calculator resides. This means that the upgrade will consume some (17K) RAM.

FIGURE 8.4
The upgraded calculator has a different "+" button and is listed as "2.0" in the About Calculator dialog box.

System Enhancements

There are several ways to modify your PalmPilot's behavior, without the overhead of a full application. This section details some third-party utilities that enhance the PalmPilot's operation.

HackMaster

HackMaster is a control application developed by Edward Keyes. This application facilitates the installation and use of system hacks, or patches—small, third-party programs that change the way the operating system works.

HackMaster implements the patch's installation and can activate or deactivate each individual patch.

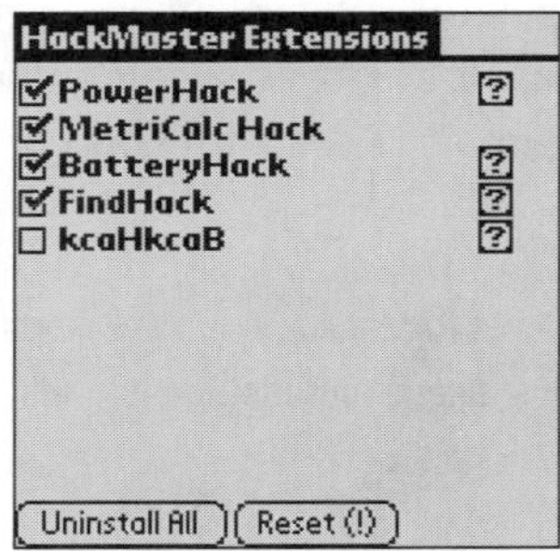

FIGURE 8.5
HackMaster coordinates, activates, and deactivates system hacks.

Along with the HackMaster program, Edward Keyes released a HackMaster API so that other developers could develop their own "hacks." Soon there were several hacks available online, such as the ones covered in the following sections.

AppHack This hack, by Edward Keyes, allows you to combine application key presses to launch up to 24 applications, instead of just four. You can define what each pair of buttons launches and a dialog box will remind you of your assignments.

BackHack This prank hack is the work of Jeff Jetton. BackHack reverses most of the words and text on your PalmPilot until you disable it.

BatteryHack DovCom's BatteryHack adds a digital battery voltage meter next to the analog meter on the Applications Launcher screen.

FIGURE 8.6
BatteryHack's digital battery meter lets you keep a closer eye on your battery's condition.

CalcHack CalcHack, by DovCom, lets you attach any application to the Calculator button. By using this hack, you can launch the calculator of your choice instead of 3Com Corporation's Calculator.

FindHack Florent Pillet's FindHack modifies the Find feature of the PalmPilot. The modified Find will locate text even if it isn't at the beginning of a word and will permit the use of question marks (?) as wild-card characters. For example, any of the following will find "Steve" when entered into the hacked Find dialog:

Steve

teve

St???

HushHack Jeff Jetton's HushHack silences the PalmPilot's alarms during serial port operations such as a HotSync. You can set HushHack to blink the screen instead of sounding the alarm if you like.

MenuHack Edward Keyes' MenuHack causes an application's menu bar to pop up when you tap its Title bar. This makes the PalmPilot menus more intuitive for users of desktop machines who aren't used to having to tap a button to get at an application's menus.

PowerHack Jack Russell's PowerHack locks the PalmPilot whenever it is turned off or turns itself off.

SilkHack SilkHack, by StingerSoft, enables you to define up to three different applications to launch by tapping the silk-screened buttons. SilkHack divides the buttons into quarters and allows you to attach an application to each quarter. Then, which application is launched depends on where you tap the buttons.

SwitchHack Murray Dowling created SwitchHack to support switching back and forth between two applications. To switch between the last two applications, draw a line from the Applications button into the Graffiti area. The PalmPilot will switch to the second application; repeating the stroke switches back to the first application.

Other Hacks

There are several other system hacks available that do not use HackMaster.

AlarmHack Wes Cherry's Alarm Hack enables you to set the system alarm to ring up to nine times longer than normal and to continually nag you until answered.

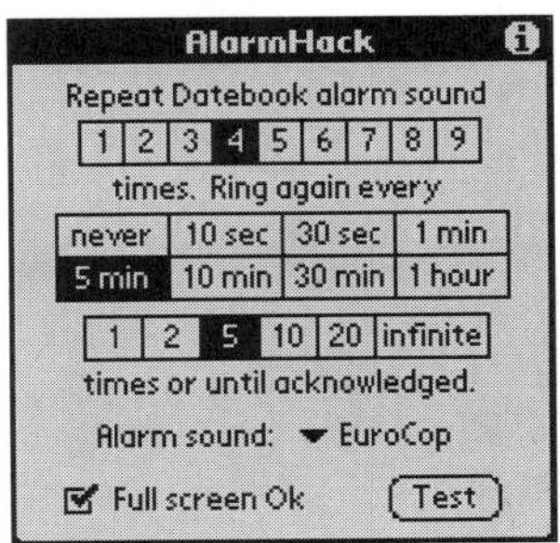

FIGURE 8.7
Set up the system alarms just the way you like them.

Check-In Check-In, by Jack Russell, provides some updated functionality to the Security Application. Check-In displays a large format clock and a custom message in case you lose your PalmPilot (someone can find you and give it back).

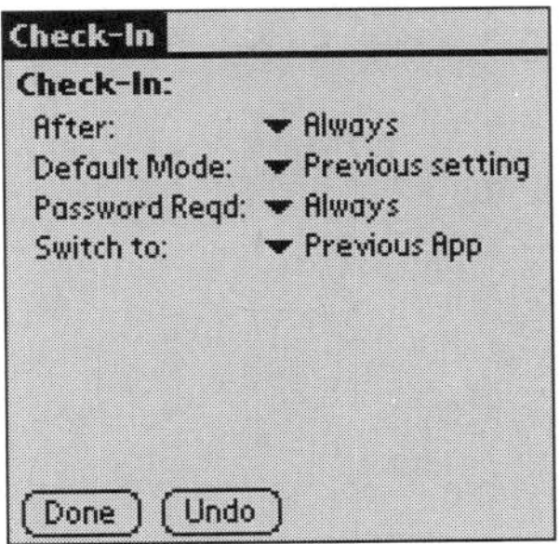

FIGURE 8.8
Check-In's password and security features can be customized to suit your needs.

Check-In also has several password options, and a counter that shows how long your PalmPilot has been on.

Volume Tan Kok Mun's Volume utility lets you explicitly set each aspect of the PalmPilot's volume. You can individually set the Master, System, and Alarm volumes and test some system sounds with your new settings.

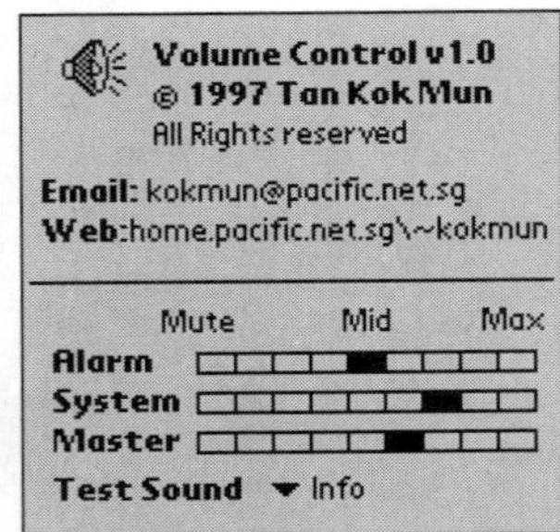

FIGURE 8.9
Customize the PalmPilot's volume to your liking.

CHAPTER 9

Developing PalmPilot Software

So you have looked everywhere for a particular piece of software for your PalmPilot, with no success? Why not create it yourself?

There are several PalmPilot applications and desktop programming utilities that will help you create your own applications. The applications you create can be as simple or as complex as you want or need—just take a look at the variety of software covered in this book!

This chapter will cover several tools that are available for creating custom programs on the PalmPilot and will show the various capabilities and limits of each tool.

NOTE This chapter will make no attempt to teach programming as that is beyond the scope of this book.

BASIC for the PalmPilot

Chipmunk BASIC is a freeware BASIC interpreter that runs on all Macintosh computers. *cbasPad*, by Ron Nicholson, brings Chipmunk BASIC to the PalmPilot.

NOTE BASIC is an acronym that stands for "Beginner's All-purpose Symbolic Instruction Code." BASIC languages are simple to learn but can be quite powerful, making them a good first choice for the beginning programmer.

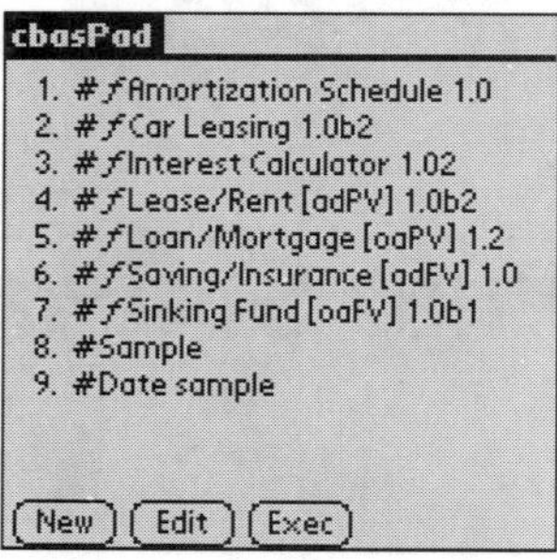

FIGURE 9.1
cbasPad uses a database-like approach, keeping all the programs together in one place, within the cbasPad interface.

cbasPad Capabilities

Actually, it's more accurate to say that Chipmunk BASIC was the inspiration for cbasPad since Ron Nicholson has done quite a bit of development to make his language more PalmPilot-friendly. Specifically, cbasPad has the following capabilities:

- Support for standard math operators, including +, -, *, /, mod, ^, =, <>, >, >=, <, <=, and, or, xor, and not.
- Standard BASIC commands, including let, print, dprint, input, if/then, for/next, gosub, return, goto, dim, float, and rem.
- Algebraic and string-handling functions, including int(), rnd(), sqr(), exp(), log(), sin(), cos(), tan(), atn(), len(), val(), str$(), chr$(), hex$(), and mid$().
- Special functions, including fre, peek(), poke, call, varptr(), eval(), fn, op, grline, dprint, sound, and sersend.

Anyone who has programmed in another BASIC language will feel right at home in cbasPad. Extra commands have been implemented to provide access to some of the PalmPilot's capabilities, like drawing lines on the screen.

cbasPad uses a Memo Pad-like editor for editing its programs. This editor also supports direct execution of individual code lines, as well as the whole program. Once a program has been entered and saved, you can select it from the main list of cbasPad's programs and execute the program directly from there.

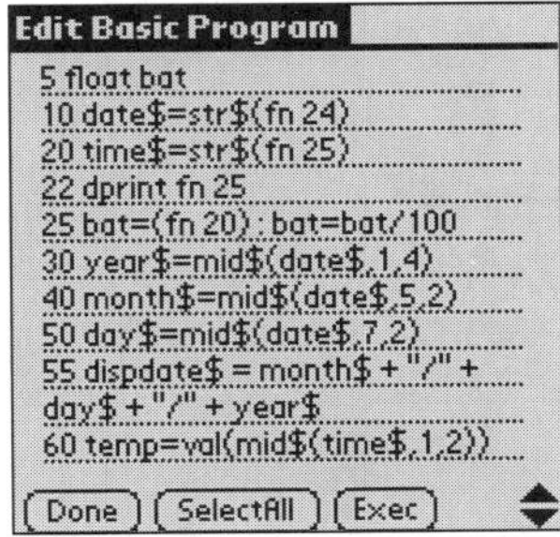

FIGURE 9.2

The cbasPad editor is full-featured, but you should opt to create most of your programs on the desktop and then HotSync them to the PalmPilot to avoid Graffiti fatigue!

Each program's executable lines should start with a `new` command and end with a `run` command—both without line numbers—for the interpreter to run the program automatically. There are exceptions to this, which are driven by programming techniques to accomplish particular tasks.

TIP Always start your program with a `REM` or # and the name of the program. This line will be used to identify your program in the main cbasPad screen.

Desktop Connectivity

Entering programming code using Graffiti can be a tedious affair. cbasPad programmers can opt to write their code on their desktop machine and then use the following procedure to get the program to the PalmPilot:

1. Import the program into the PalmPilot Desktop's Memo Pad.
2. HotSync the memo to the PalmPilot.
3. Use the PalmPilot's clipboard to cut and paste the code from Memo Pad into cbasPad.

Alternatively, you can use Tan Kok Mun's cbasPDB program to insert your programs into the cbasPad database directly. The database is backed up to your PalmPilot with every HotSync; look for it in the PalmPilot's Install directory (cbasDB.PDB).

> **CAUTION** Never use the Install Application program to install another cbasPad PDB file without combining it with your backup database. Doing so will replace all of your cbasPad programs with the programs in the new PDB.

Sample Programs and Uses

The commands used in cbasPad to utilize the Graffiti pad and the touch screen are some of the most-used commands in the language. These commands and functions are specific to the PalmPilot—they use specific memory locations to gather information about the PalmPilot and to toggle PalmPilot functions.

The `fn` command is used to access PalmPilot functions. This command takes a number parameter corresponding to the desired function. For example, `fn 33` retrieves the next character entered on the Graffiti pad, `fn 16` returns the value of a seconds timer, and `fn 24` returns the current date as a number. Using the `op` command, you can draw characters on-screen, and even read from the Memo Pad and Address Book databases.

These functions are simple to implement. For example, the following small program accepts one character from the Graffiti pad and displays it in a dialog box:

```
#Get one Graffiti Character
new
10 c=fn 33
20 dprint "Character: ",chr$(c)
run
```

The following example is quite a bit more involved, using the functions to retrieve and display the current date, time, and battery power. Note that this example shows how rough function data can be, but also how rich the cbasPad BASIC functions are (especially string handling functions).

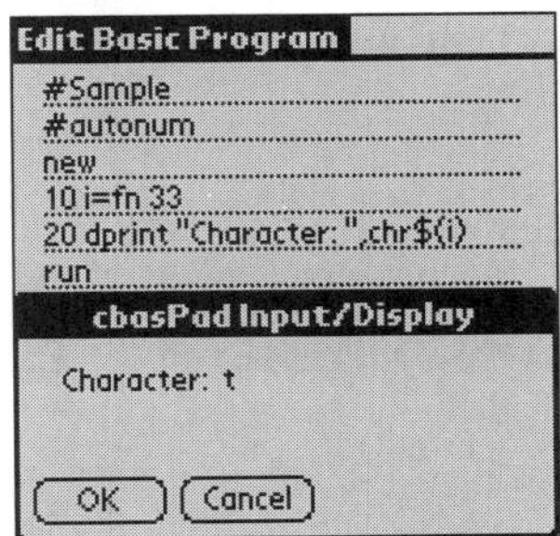

FIGURE 9.3

Getting characters from the Graffiti pad and displaying them is an easy task.

```
# Date/Time/Battery display
new
# Define vars
10 float bat
# Get date, time, and battery level
20 date$ = str$(fn 24)
30 time$ = str$(fn 25)
35 if len(time$)<6 then time$="0"+time$ : goto 36
40 bat = fn 20 : bat = bat/100
# Break down date
50 year$ = mid$(date$,1,4)
60 month$ = mid$(date$,5,2)
70 day$ = mid$(date$,7,2)
80 dispdate$ = month$ + "/" + day$ +"/"+year$
# Get hour in 12hr am/pm format
90 temp = val(mid$(time$,1,2))
100 ampm$ = " am  "
110 if temp<13 then goto 140
120 ampm$ = " pm  "
130 temp = temp-12
140 if temp = 0 then temp = 12
# Set up date display (HH:MM am/pm)
150 t$ = str$(temp) : t = len(t$)-2
160 disptime$ = mid$(t$,1,t) + ":"
170 disptime$ = disptime$ + mid$(time$,3,2) + ampm$
# Set up final display "MM/DD/YY, HH:MM am/pm  (N v)"
180 disp$ = dispdate$ + ", " + disptime$
190 disp$ = disp$ + "( " + str$(bat) + "v)"
# Display dialog
200 dprint disp$
run
```

There are several dozen programs available online that use cbasPad. Some of the more popular include:

- A battery meter that shows actual volts
- A game of Tic-Tac-Toe
- A program to graph user-defined functions
- A Morse Code tutor
- A full-featured Musicbox for creating music on the PalmPilot
- A currency converter

You can find many cbasPad programs on Tan Kok Mun's PalmPilot BASIC Web page, **home.pacific.net.sg/~kokmun/basic.htm**.

CASL

The *Compact Application Solution Language* (CASL), by Feras Information Technologies, is an event-driven language for the PalmPilot. There are several things that make CASL unique:

- CASL can compile programs to run on Windows, as well as on the PalmPilot
- The CASL Integrated Development Environment (IDE) can compile directly to PRC files, which can be directly HotSynced to the PalmPilot
- CASL is GUI in nature, allowing the construction and display of custom dialog boxes and windows
- Being event driven, CASL programs respond more dynamically to user interaction
- CASL supports "Packages," related code that can be stored in a file and included in other programs with one statement, "Include" (much like Libraries in some programming languages)
- CASL programs are compiled into p-code and executed by a run-time module

NOTE CASL is shareware. The demo copy is full-featured but only enables you to compile small programs with a limited number of variables. The registered version is $64.95 and can be purchased by calling or faxing Feras Technologies. Check out the details on the CASL Web page: **www.caslsoft.com**.

The CASL Development Environment

The heart of CASL is the IDE, where you develop, compile, test, and troubleshoot programs. The IDE includes a full-featured text editor, including a multiple document interface, full search-and-replace capability, and the capability to print.

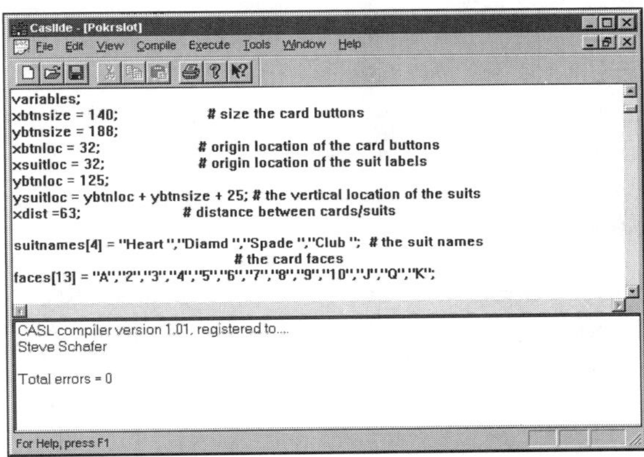

FIGURE 9.4
Create, edit, compile, and run your program from within the CASL IDE.

After writing your program, you can compile it for Windows or the PalmPilot. The IDE will inform you of any errors or will indicate a successful program compilation.

TIP Clicking any error message will take you directly to the offending line so you can fix the problem.

Selecting Run from the Execute menu will run the current program in Windows, where you can test its operation before porting it to the PalmPilot. When your application is ready for the PalmPilot, compile it by using the PalmPilot option on the Compile menu. Then, choose Make PRC from the Compile menu to make a PRC file, ready to install on the PalmPilot. The IDE also includes an Install PRC option that will automatically launch the PalmPilot's Install Application program, specifying the new PRC. All you need to do is HotSync.

TIP You can run a CASL program in Windows without the IDE by executing the CASLWin program and specifying the appropriate compiled CSP file. Consider creating a shortcut that you can place on the desktop or on the Start Menu.

Programming with CASL

The CASL language is straightforward; you define objects and functions to act upon them. The language does follow its own syntax, but that syntax is relatively easy to learn. Remember that all containers must have an "end" statement, each individual statement needs to end in a semicolon (;), and that you need to explicitly declare all your variables.

As stated, CASL is event driven. Each object you create can cause a function to be executed when it is acted upon and, in turn, the function can modify the object. For example, if you want to define a button, you use code similar to:

```
button button_name;
       position x, y;
       display "text";
end;

function function_name;
       ...function code...
end;
```

Note that the button is linked to the function by having the same name; that is, *button_name* and *function_name* are the same. The "button" container defines where the button will be placed on the screen (by the x and y values) and what the button will say ("text"). When the button is pressed, the corresponding function is executed.

Besides buttons, CASL supports the following objects:

- Pop-up menus
- Scroll lists
- File name lists
- Text fields
- Static text

- Frames (dialogs and windows)
- Files
- Databases

Each visual object has properties that control its position on the screen and its general behavior. File, database, and list objects include additional properties that control their content. Functions can directly modify objects and call other functions. There is a `timer` function that can be used to call a function at a certain time. CASL also includes several functions to manipulate strings and numbers, retrieve the current time and date, and more.

Files and databases are easily created and managed with CASL—you can use CASL to quickly create a form-entry database if you want. The CASL package comes with an example database program to get you started.

FIGURE 9.5
Form-driven databases are a good use for CASL.

Creating CASL programs is easy and straightforward. Simply create your objects on the display and then write functions to handle them. For example, this code creates a simple stopwatch that displays the current time and includes start, stop, and reset functions.

```
#
# A simple stopwatch program
#
variables;
        temphour=0;
        ampm="am";
```

```
        timrflag=0;
        timrmin=0;
        timrsec=0;
end;

# Show the current time here
label the_time;
        position 100,200;
end;

# Show the timer (stopwatch) here
label tmr_txt;
        position 100,300;
end;

# Define our start/stop and reset buttons
button startnstop;
        position 100,500;
        display "Start";
end;

button reset_timer;
        position 430,500;
        display "Reset";
end;

# Function fires every second, to display the current time
➥and timer (if active)
function clock_tick;
        ampm="am";
        temphour=hour();
        if temphour > 12;
                ampm="pm";
                temphour=temphour - 12;
        end_if;
        put the_time,  "Current Time:  "+
string(temphour,"0#") + ":" +
string(minute(),"0#")+":"+string(second(),"0#")+ "   " + ampm;
        if timrflag=1;
                timrsec=timrsec + 1;
                if timrsec>60;
                        timrsec=0;
                        timrmin=timrmin+1;
                end_if;
                put tmr_txt, string(timrmin,"0#")+" :
"+string(timrsec,"0#");
        end_if;
        timer clock_tick, 1000;
end;

# Start/Stop button
function startnstop;
        if timrflag=1;
```

```
            put tmr_txt,  string(timrmin,"0#")+" :
➥"+string(timrsec,"0#");
            timrflag=0;
            put startnstop, "Start";
      else;
            put tmr_txt,  string(timrmin,"0#")+" :
➥"+string(timrsec,"0#");
            timrflag=1;
            put startnstop, "Stop";
      end_if;
end;

# Reset button
function reset_timer;
      timrsec=0;
      timrmin=0;
      put tmr_txt,  string(timrmin,"0#")+" :
➥"+string(timrsec,"0#");
end;

# Initializes values and starts the clock_tick function loop
function startup;
      timrflag=1;
      timer startnstop, 0;
      timer clock_tick, 1000;
end;
```

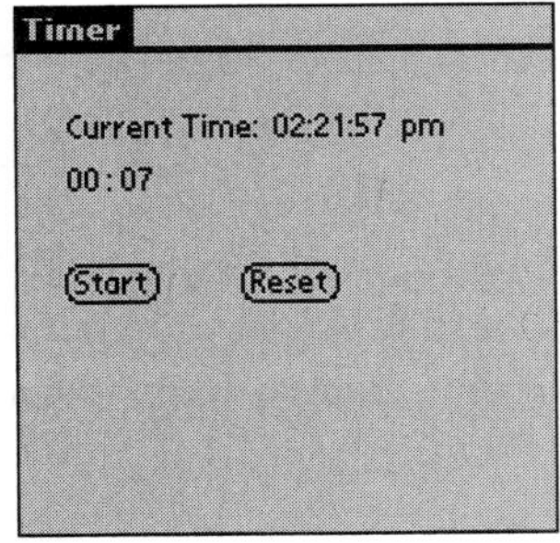

FIGURE 9.6
This stopwatch program uses timed events and dynamic buttons.

NOTE This sample program is provided to show some of CASL's capabilities, but is too large to compile with the demo copy of CASL.

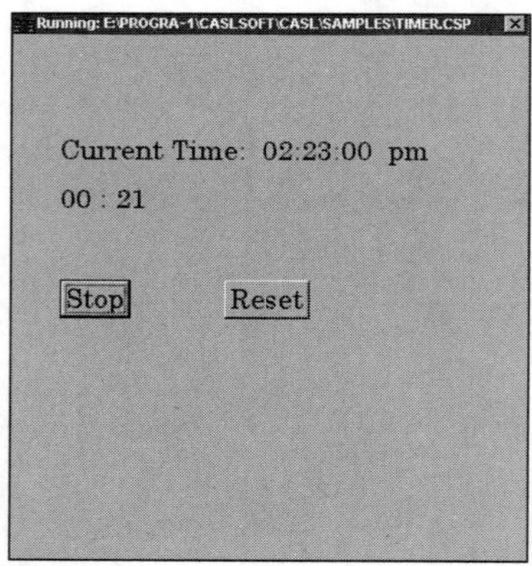

FIGURE 9.7
The current time (and timer value) is displayed every second and the Start/Stop button changes its text dynamically. Note that this figure shows the same application running in Windows.

John Feras and the crew at Feras Technologies have been busy developing special CASL packages (CPKs) to interact with the PalmPilot's databases. Currently, there is a CPK for the Memo Pad, Address Book, and To Do List. Check the CASL Web page (**www.caslsoft. com**) in the near future for more packages and code examples.

To install CASL programs on your PalmPilot, you first need to install CASLRT.PRC (the run-time interpreter). Then, use the IDE to compile your program to a PRC file and install it. The program will show up in the Application Launcher with the name you gave it and the CASL icon.

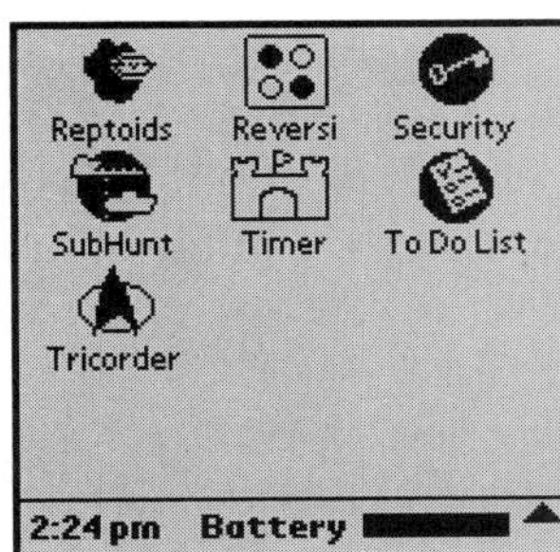

FIGURE 9.8
Your programs (and their data) are stored separately and show up with their own icons in the Application Launcher.

Jump—Java for the PalmPilot

Jump, by Greg Hewgill, is a PC-based program that enables you to use the Java programming language to write PalmPilot applications. Jump compiles your Java code into a 68000-compatible assembly-language (ASM) file. You then can use an assembly-language compiler such as Pila to compile the ASM file to a PRC.

NOTE See the section, "The Alternate SDK," later in this chapter, for more information on Pila and other PalmPilot tools.

Jump is freeware, available to all developers who want to use it. However, Jump is not for the faint-hearted or the non-Java-aware user. There are a lot of prerequisites before you can create a PalmPilot application with Jump, including the installation of a full Java Development Package and a deep understanding of the Java language.

TIP Explore more about Jump on Greg Hewgill's Jump Web page at **userzweb.lightspeed.net/~gregh/pilot/jump/**.

Utilizing Java Tools

Coding and compiling is done using a third-party Java SDK, such as Sun's or Microsoft's, along with Jump's PalmPilot libraries. You run Jump on your main Class file—it creates an ASM file and automatically runs Pila to compile the file into a PRC.

NOTE Jump requires that you have a function titled `PilotMain` in your main class file. Jump will set up this function to be called when your program is run. The declaration resembles:

```
public static int PilotMain(int cmd, int cmdPBP,
➥int launchFlags)
```

Resources for the program are stored in a *classname*.res, where *classname* is the name of the main class you ran through Jump. ■

Jump comes with a multitude of classes for controlling the PalmPilot, making interaction with the PalmPilot's OS easier.

NOTE You can find the Javasoft Java SDK on the Web at **www.javasoft.com** and the Microsoft Java SDK at **www.microsoft.com/msdownload/javasdk/01000.htm**. Jump requires the classes and compiler from either of these packages to compile your Java programs. ■

You should understand that Jump does not bring Java directly to the PalmPilot. It simply allows you to use the Java language as a basis for programming the PalmPilot. You still won't be able to run that "dancing letter" Java application on the PalmPilot!

It Does Look Like Java

One look at a Jump program will show just how Java-like the programs can be. The following example is a standard programmer's "Hello World" sample program from the Jump package:

```
import palmos.*;

class Hello {
  static final int idfMain = 1000;

  public static int PilotMain(int cmd, int cmdBPB, int
➥launchFlags)
  {
```

```
    if (cmd != 0) {
      return 0;
    }

    frm.FrmGotoForm(idfMain);

    Event e = new Event();
    Short err = new Short();
    while (e.eType != Event.appStopEvent) {
      evt.EvtGetEvent(e, -1);
      if (!sys.SysHandleEvent(e)) {
        if (!menu.MenuHandleEvent(0, e, err)) {
          if (!appHandleEvent(e)) {
            frm.FrmHandleEvent(frm.FrmGetActiveForm(), e);
          }
        }
      }
    }

    return 0;
  }

  static boolean appHandleEvent(Event e)
  {
    if (e.eType == Event.frmLoadEvent) {
      int form = frm.FrmInitForm(e.formID());
      frm.FrmSetActiveForm(form);
      return true;
    } else if (e.eType == Event.frmOpenEvent) {
      frm.FrmDrawForm(frm.FrmGetActiveForm());
      return true;
    }
    return false;
  }
}
```

When this program is compiled and run on the PalmPilot, it resembles any other PalmPilot application, complete with its own Application Launcher icon.

GCC for the PalmPilot

John J. Lehett has created a version of GNU C (GCC) to create PalmPilot applications under Windows 32. GNU C is a variant of the C programming language that is popular on Unix computers. As of this writing, the language was still in development, but is gaining popularity. For more information, see the GCC Win32 Port Web page at **www.ftpx.com/pilotgcc/gccwin32.html**.

Metrowerks' *CodeWarrior*

The crème de la crème of the PalmPilot programming crowd is Metrowerks' CodeWarrior for the PalmPilot. Metrowerks' products were used to program the original PalmPilot OS and its built-in applications.

What Is CodeWarrior?

Metrowerks' programming tools are well-known and respected in the Macintosh programming world, and their new CodeWarrior for the PalmPilot brings Metrowerks' programming tools to the PalmPilot-development public.

Note that CodeWarrior isn't for hobbyists—it is a full-retail package costing several hundred dollars. However, if you are serious about your applications, CodeWarrior is hard to beat.

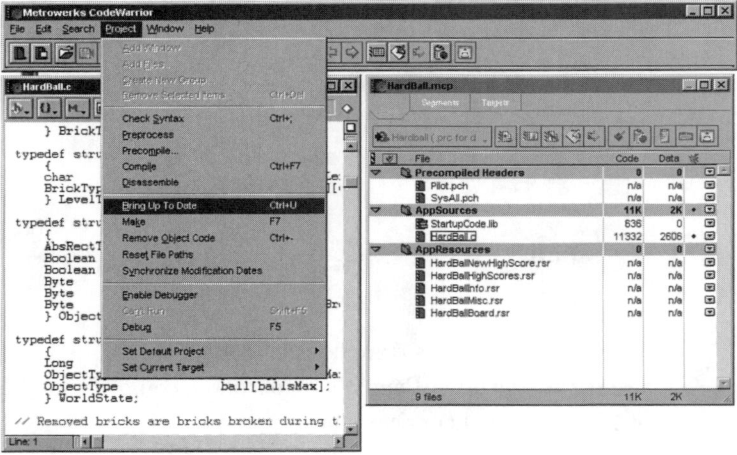

FIGURE 9.9
Metrowerks' CodeWarrior is a full-fledged programming environment with professional tools for code development.

Metrowerks' CodeWarrior Professional product supports C, C++, Pascal, and Java on the Mac and PC. CodeWarrior for the PalmPilot only supports C and runs on a Mac or PC. The current version (Developer Release 2, DR2) provides extra tools for the Mac platform, such as the Pilot Simulator, which can be used to test your programs before installing them on a real PalmPilot.

NOTE Metrowerks' CodeWarrior for the PalmPilot bundle comes with a PalmPilot Personal or Professional for development use.

What Do You Mean: "For the PalmPilot"?

CodeWarrior for the PalmPilot is tailored specifically for creating applications for the PalmPilot. The underlying application and support programs are the same as those in other CodeWarrior products. However, this package includes libraries, source, and examples to create PalmPilot-ready applications. The Mac version currently comes with a Pilot Simulator, enabling you to run your programs on the simulator before installing them on a real PalmPilot.

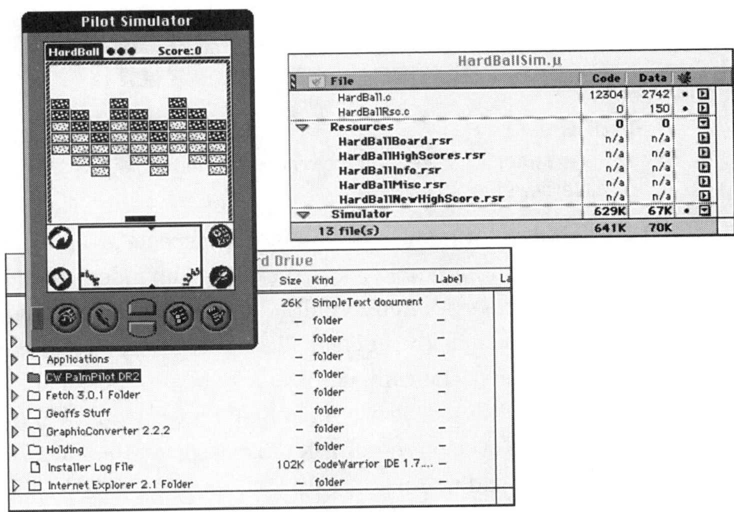

FIGURE 9.10
The Pilot Simulator lets you test your applications with full debug capability before loading them on your PalmPilot.

NOTE The next version of CodeWarrior for the PalmPilot will include more troubleshooting applications and utilities for Windows, duplicating Mac tools such as the Pilot Simulator.

CodeWarrior for the PalmPilot also includes tools for building your own conduits and desktop computer-support programs, so you can HotSync data created by your programs to and from the desktop.

The CodeWarrior Interface

The CodeWarrior interface follows the multiple-window model, opening new program windows as needed for project management, program compilation, and so forth.

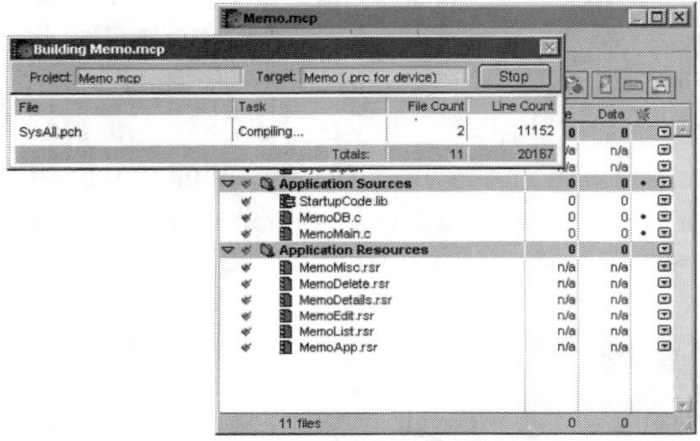

FIGURE 9.11
The CodeWarrior IDE uses separate windows for individual tasks and code views.

By using these windows, you can see all aspects of a project, or an individual program. Resources can be built independently and linked into projects where required. Comprehensive debugging utilities let you quickly find and eliminate any problems, wherever they might hide. The compiler is quick and produces PalmPilot-ready files (PRCs). A bevy of PalmPilot-specific tools and examples enable you to create programs for execution on the PalmPilot, external conduits, and more.

As previously mentioned, CodeWarrior is not for the casual programmer. Although worthy of far more coverage than is presented here, fully exploring CodeWarrior is beyond the scope of this chapter. However, for the professional code developer, there are no finer tools available for PalmPilot development.

Other PalmPilot Development Tools

There are a few public-domain development tools available for the PalmPilot. This section highlights the most popular tools available.

CoPilot PalmPilot Emulator

Greg Hewgill's CoPilot is one of the premier tools for PalmPilot developers. The CoPilot is a PalmPilot-emulation program that runs on a desktop machine and is capable of executing any program that can run on a PalmPilot.

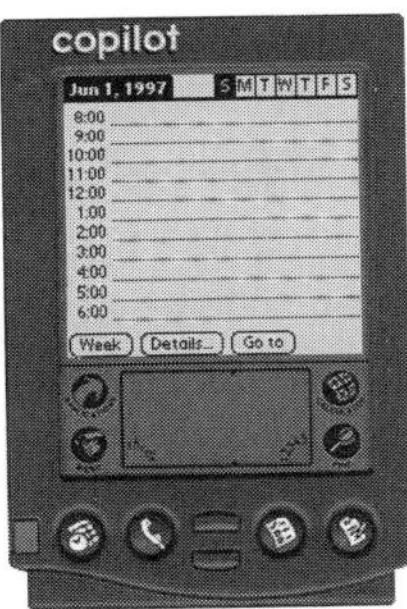

FIGURE 9.12
CoPilot, by Greg Hewgill, is a must for PalmPilot developers and users alike.

TIP Besides providing a tool for developers, CoPilot also can be a useful companion for any PalmPilot user. Before taking up valuable space on your PalmPilot, load an application on the CoPilot and experiment with it a bit. If you like what you see, you can then HotSync the application to the real PalmPilot.

NOTE CoPilot was developed mainly for the Windows 95 platform, but a Mac version has recently been released, as well as the source code for Unix, Linux, and other operating systems.

At its simplest level, CoPilot is a 68328 processor emulator that is tied to a software simulation of the PalmPilot's hardware. CoPilot uses a dynamic file to simulate the PalmPilot's RAM. For the ROM, CoPilot requires that you run a special application on your PalmPilot that exports the ROM to your desktop computer for CoPilot's use.

NOTE As Greg Hewgill admits, "Use of the GetRom program may place you in violation of your license agreement with U.S. Robotics. Please read page 123 of your Pilot handbook ("Software License Agreement") before running GetRom." (See the Software License Agreement in your PalmPilot Handbook.)

NOTE As of this writing, CoPilot is not compatible with the PalmPilot 1 megabyte ROM (Personal and Professional). A new version of the CoPilot that does support OS 2.x is in beta test as this text is being written. Check out Greg's Web site for more information (**userzweb.lightspeed.net/~gregh/pilot/copilot/index.html**).

Installing applications and databases on the CoPilot couldn't be easier—just right-click the CoPilot to bring up the control menu, choose Load App, and select the file you want to load. There is also a Reset menu choice for performing a soft reset on the CoPilot.

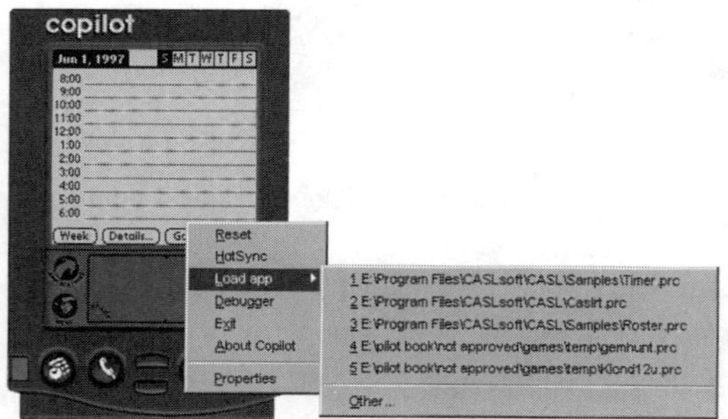

FIGURE 9.13
Loading applications is menu-driven on the CoPilot, providing quick access to sample or test applications.

CoPilot uses the desktop machine's serial port as its serial port, allowing access to any serial device attached to the computer. If you connect two serial ports via a null modem cable, you can also use HotSync with the CoPilot, with the CoPilot using one port and the HotSync Manager using the other.

CoPilot really excels with its debug function. This function provides a debugging window where you can tinker with the RAM and ROM, exposing register settings and memory contents.

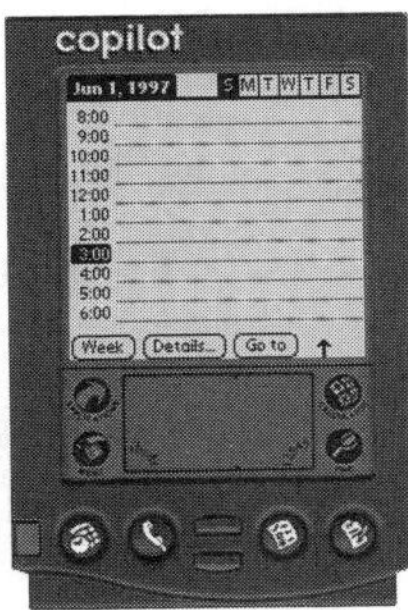

FIGURE 9.14
The CoPilot debugger lets you see the inside of the code, OS, and memory.

The *Alternate Software Development Kit*

Shortly after the Pilot 1000's release, U.S. Robotics released a Software Development Kit for the Macintosh. This kit allowed developers to create applications, conduits, and utilities for the Pilot 1000, but only on the Mac. The SDK included Metrowerks' CodeWarrior package and, upon its release, retailed for about $500.

With no release of a comparable kit for the PC in sight, several third-party developers came up with their own, the Alternate Software Developer's Kit (ASDK). The ASDK contains the following tools:

- 68328 cross-assembler (Pila)
- PalmPilot resource compiler and previewer (PilRC, PilRCUI)
- PalmPilot emulator and debugger (CoPilot)
- 68328 disassembler (PilDis)
- PalmPilot API documentation (PilotAPI.hlp)
- 3Com Corporation SDK header files
- Miscellaneous support utilities (exe2prc, PilotHack, prc2bin, prc2bmp)
- Sample programs

These utilities were developed by the following individuals:

Wes Cherry	PilRC, PilRCUI, Pila enhancements, HackMaster sample
Greg Hewgill	CoPilot, getrom
Bill Hunt	PilDis
Scott Ludwig	prc2bmp, exe2prc enhancements
Darrin Massena	Pila, exe2prc, PilotHack, prc2bin, ASDK organization
Matt Peterson	PilotAPI.hlp
3Com Corporation	SDK C header files, MemoPad sample

Darrin Massena is the main force behind the ASDK and he keeps it updated and maintains the relationship with 3Com Corporation. These utilities make it easier for developers working on the PC platform to design, write, troubleshoot, and publish PalmPilot applications.

Detailing the ASDK is well beyond the scope of this chapter, but the intrepid programmer can use these utilities to accomplish many development tasks. Those wanting more details on the ASDK should review Darrin Massena's ASDK Web page at **www.massena.com/darrin/pilot/index.html**.

Pilot Studio

Some users may be dismayed by the lack of synergy between the tools provided in the PalmPilot ASDK. Those users should check out Pilot Studio, by Alain Falanga. Pilot Studio is a freeware IDE for the ASDK, Jump, and your favorite Java compiler.

When you install Pilot Studio, you specify where all the ASDK and Jump tools are located so that you can access them through the Studio's interface. Pilot Studio itself offers a text and project editor, as well as menus with options to most ASDK, Jump, and Java tools.

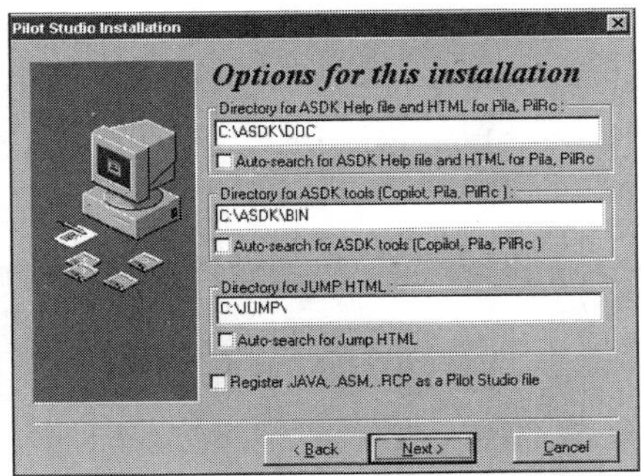

FIGURE 9.15
Enter the location(s) for the ASDK and other tools during Pilot Studio's setup.

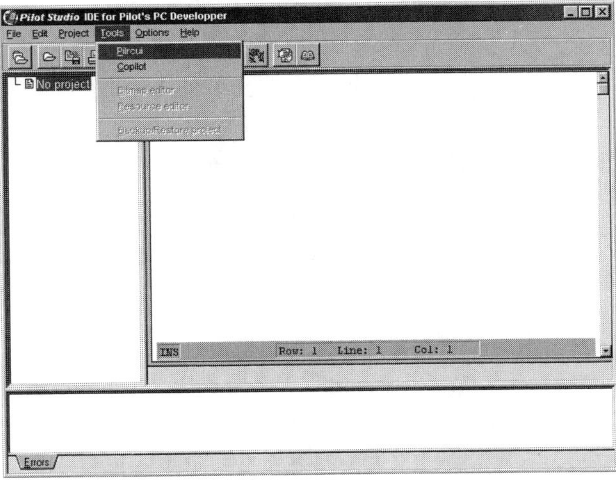

FIGURE 9.16
The IDE looks familiar to software developers, with easy access to the ASDK and other tools.

The ability to access the ASDK tools from an integrated menu makes program development and troubleshooting easier. As of this writing, Pilot Studio was still in testing with a pre-release version available from Adam's PalmPilot Software Archive on the Web (**Home.InfoRamp.Net/~adam/pilot/**). Keep an eye on this site for future releases of the Pilot Studio.

PilotIconEditor

Every good PalmPilot program needs a flashy icon for the Application Launcher screen. That's where the PilotIconEditor by Brad Goodman comes in handy.

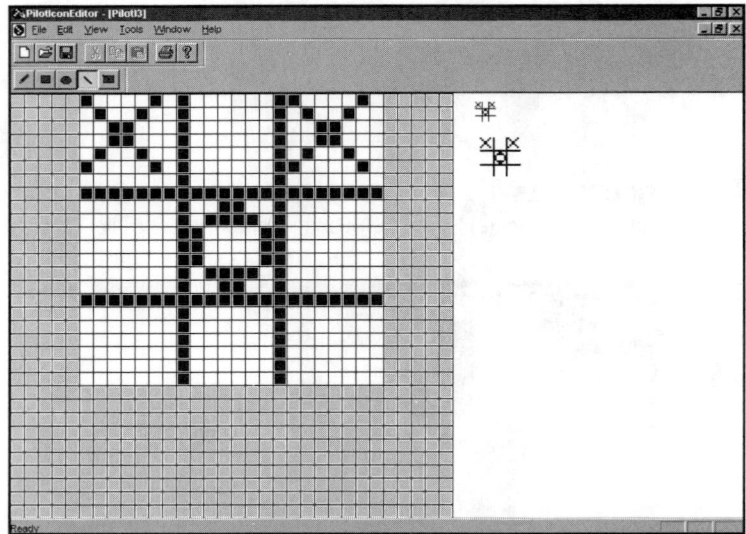

FIGURE 9.17
Use the PilotIconEditor to create custom icons for your programs.

The PilotIconEditor runs under Windows and can quickly create an icon for your application. You can pull icons out of PRCs by using prc2bin (from the ASDK) and then edit it with the PilotIconEditor.

TIP You also can use prc2bmp to export icons from PRCs and then edit them with any Windows bitmap editor.

PalmPilot Resources

There are many resources upon which the PalmPilot user and developer can rely, from 3Com Corporation-sponsored Web sites and customer support, to third-party development tools. This Appendix provides a guide to some of the best resources available for the PalmPilot.

NOTE New resources are created online almost on a daily basis. Check your favorite Web/online search engine periodically to update this list.

3Com Corporation/Palm Computing, Inc.

3Com Corporation/Palm Computing, Inc. can be reached at the following address:

3Com Corporation/Palm Computing, Inc.
1565 Charleston Road
Mountain View, CA 94043-9450

Product and Customer Support

Product Information/Orders: 800-881-Palm (800-881-7256)

Faxback Service: 847-762-6163

Customer Service: 888-619-7488

Technical Support and Repair

Technical Support or Repair: 847-676-1441 (8 A.M.—6 P.M., M-F, CST)

Technical Support or Repair Fax: 847-676-7323

Accessories

Accessories (US): 800-881-7256

Accessories (outside US): 408-848-5604

UK Support

Internet e-mail: **uksupport@usr.com**

BBS: 0118 969 2200

Faxback: 0118 922 8299

Fax: 0118 969 4222

Telephone: 0118 944 1000

US Bulletin Board

847-982-5092 (PC Board, 33.6 access)

Internet

Main Web Page: **www.usr.com/palm**

Support Pages: **www.usr.com/palm/support**

E-mail: **support@palm.usr.com**

PalmPilot News Groups:

- **alt.comp.sys.palmtops.pilot**
- **comp.sys.palmtops**
- **comp.sys.handhelds**
- **comp.sys.pen**

AOL

Keyword: PalmPilot

Lots of sections containing information, patches and upgrades, add-on software, and more.

CompuServe

Palmtop B Forum (**GO PALMB**)

Section/Library 5 (PalmPilot Official) has all the updates, patches, and support files from 3Com Corporation.

Section/Library 8 (PalmPilot Unofficial) has many of the add-on products and development tools.

Third-Party Online Resources

There are many places to go for support and additional PalmPilot applications. In fact, the majority of these resources are not associated with 3Com Corporation—they are created by other PalmPilot users and third-party developers.

Add-On Software Web Sites

There are a few main Web sites where you can find virtually any third-party add-on for the PalmPilot.

StingerSoft URL: **pilot.cc-inc.com/stinger/stingersoft.cfm**

The largest, most up-to-date collection of PalmPilot software available. Also has current PalmPilot news, tips, etc.

Adam's PalmPilot Software Archive URL: **Home.InfoRamp.Net/~adam/pilot/**

Another large, up-to-date collection of PalmPilot software. Also has links to other useful PalmPilot sites.

Andy's PalmPilot Page URL: **www.bconnex.net/~atane/**

An index to PalmPilot developers and their products.

Information Locations and Sites

Besides additional software, there is a wealth of information available about the PalmPilot. This section highlights the most valuable resources available.

Calvin's PalmPilot FAQ URL: **www.pilotfaq.com**

Frequently Asked Questions about the 3Com Corporation PalmPilot products. A great source of information.

PalmPilot Web Ring URL: **pilot.cc-inc.com/webring/**

A "ring" of Web sites, each with buttons to move to the next site or the previous site.

PalmPilot Mailing Lists A high-traffic mail list frequented by users and developers. Subscribe to the list or the list digest by sending a message to **pilot-request@sundog.ultraviolet.org** with either:

> **Subscribe Pilot <your email address>**
> or
> **Subscribe Pilot-Digest <your email address>**

as the body of the message.

TIP The mailing list easily generates 30-60 messages a day. Use your mail program's rules or filtering capability to place all the messages in a separate folder, or subscribe to the digest instead.

Software Development Sites

If you are looking for information about developing PalmPilot add-ons, you will find a lot of information online. This section highlights some of the most valuable resources available.

Metrowerks, Inc. URL: **www.metrowerks.com**

Makers of the popular Code Warrior for PalmPilot, both Mac and Windows versions.

PalmPilot Development Tools URL: **userzweb.lightspeed.net/~gregh/pilot**

Home of CoPilot (the Windows PalmPilot emulator) and Jump (the Java-like PalmPilot language).

PalmPilot Software Development URL:**www.massena.com/darrin/pilot/index.html**

Various PalmPilot software-development tools, including the Alternate Software Development Kit (ASDK), PalmPilot Resource Compiler (PilRC), and more.

GCCPilot Page URL: **www.ftpx.com/pilotgcc/gccwin32.html**

A special version of the popular GCC language for PalmPilot development.

PalmPilot Development Mailing List There is a special mailing list available for PalmPilot developers. The list is a public setting for developers to share ideas and to gain insights from 3Com Corporation on developing applications for the PalmPilot.

Because the list is sponsored by 3Com Corporation, you must contact them to get access to the list. If you want to be considered for the list, send a message to **devsupp@palm.com**.

APPENDIX B

Software Compendium

This book includes a CD-ROM containing some of the best applications available for the PalmPilot. There are even more applications available online. The following pages detail software applications that are available for the PalmPilot online and those applications that also are included on the CD.

Using the CD-ROM

Use of the CD-ROM is straightforward; each program is stored in its own subdirectory. Simply put the CD in the CD-ROM drive of your desktop computer and use the Install Application program to install the applications on your PalmPilot. Desktop applications generally can be run directly from the CD.

NOTE All applicable documentation and support files can also be found in the application's subdirectory. See the README file on the CD-ROM for a guide to the exact location and organization of the software on the CD-ROM.

App Name	Category	Description
4-in-a-Line	Entertainment	Try to get four game pieces in a row.
8 Ball	Entertainment	Magic 8-Ball answers yes or no questions.
Abacus Financial Calc	Calculator	Calculator with financial functions.
Abroad!	Calculator	World time and currency converter.
AccessIt!	E-mail/Terminal	Enhanced version of SimpleTerm.
Agenda	Productivity	Display your appointments and To Do items for the week.
Air for RPN	Calculator	Adds currency exchange, world time display, timers, music player, and a MasterMind-like game to the RPN calculator.
AlarmHack	Enhancement	Change the tone and duration of the PalmPilot's default alarm.
Alternate Software Development Kit (ASDK)	Programming	All the tools necessary for creating PalmPilot applications on the PC.
Analog Clock	Clock	Simple analog clock.
BackHack	Enhancement	Change PalmPilot's text to read backwards. (Gimmick/Prank)
Ball	Entertainment	Softball scorekeeper.
Birthdate	Calendar	Keeps track of birthdays with reminders.
BlackBox	Entertainment	Strategy game, find gems by shooting lasers.
BlackJack	Entertainment	PalmPilot version of card game.
BMeter	Enhancement	Displays battery voltage.

Online Source	Memory Required	On the CD?
home1.pacific.net.sg/~kokmun/pilotpgm.htm	21K	✓
www.arkwin.com/flip/flip.html	10K	
www.dovcom.com/	19K	✓
Home.InfoRamp.Net/~adam/pilot/about/4.txt	34K	✓
www.tt.rim.or.jp/~tatsushi/	10K	
www.dovcom.com/	19K	✓
www.item.ntnu.no/~csurgay/pilot/air/air.html	6K	✓
www.scumby.com/scumbysoft/pilot/	7K	
www.massena.com/darrin/pilot/asdk/asdknews.htm	n/a	
www.isi.edu/~carlton/pilot	7K	
www.mindspring.com/~jetton/pilot/index.html	2K	✓
198.70.114.128/stinger/stingersoft.cfm	18K	✓
stirling.tzl.de/pilot/	31K	✓
www.dovcom.com/	9K	✓
www.RedtailSoft.com/	26K	✓
www.dovcom.com/	5K	✓

continues

SOFTWARE COMPENDIUM

continued

App Name	Category	Description
Buffalo Girls	Electronic Text & Utils	Electronic book.
CalcCOOLator	Calculator	Calculator with multiple registers.
CASL	Programming	Object-oriented programming for PalmPilot.
cbasPad	Programming	Integer BASIC for PalmPilot.
cbasPDB	Programming	Utility to turn text files into cbasPad files.
CheckIn	Enhancement	Locks PalmPilot upon power off—displays owner's name and contact information upon powerup, with optional password.
Chess	Entertainment	Full-featured electronic chess for PalmPilot.
Crossbow	Entertainment	Electronic crossword puzzles.
CurrCalc	Calculator	Calculate currency exchanges.
DigiClock	Clock	Simple digital clock.
DigiPet	Entertainment	Electronic pet.
DinkyPad	Graphics	Full featured bitmap drawing program.
Doodle	Graphics	Draw simple freehand figures on your PalmPilot.
Expense Reporter (demo)	Productivity	Track expenses.
Fax	E-mail/Terminal	Fax using a faxmodem attached to PalmPilot.
FindHack	Enhancement	Allows searching for text within words.
FinFunctions for RPN	Financial	Financial functions for the RPN calculator.

Online Source	Memory Required	On the CD?
www.jitterbug.com/pages/buffalo.html	181K (10 × 13-26K)	✓
www.cs.unibo.it/~fabio/pilot.html	13K	
www.caslsoft.com	28K	✓
www.nicholson.com/rhn/pilot.html	40K	
home.pacific.net.sg/~kokmun/basic.htm	n/a	✓
dialspace.dial.pipex.com/jakr/pilot	15K	✓
www.eskimo.com/~scottlu/pilot/	28K	
wr.com.au/harryo/crossbow/	16K	
Home.InfoRamp.Net/~adam/pilot	16K	✓
198.70.114.128/stinger/stingersoft.cfm	4K	
www.wakuwaku.or.jp/shuji/	20K	
www.1stresource.com/~mistered/dinkypad.htm	20K	
www.elf.org/pilot/doodle.html	6K	
www.iambic.com	n/a	
Home.InfoRamp.Net/~adam/pilot	34K	
w3.teaser.fr/~fpillet/pilot/	2K	✓
www.pipeline.com/~benjam	1K	✓

continues

continued

App Name	Category	Description
FlipIt	Entertainment	Strategy game, turn all the squares to black.
FreeCell	Entertainment	PalmPilot version of card game.
Game Pack	Entertainment	Four games from 3Com Corporation: Hard Ball, MineHunt, Puzzle, and Sub Hunt.
GemHunt	Entertainment	Strategy game, find gems by shooting lasers.
Generic Conduit Manager	PC Utilities	Install third-party conduits into HotSync Manager 1.1.
GraffitiHelp	Enhancement	Displays Graffiti strokes for characters.
GuessMe	Entertainment	MasterMind-like game.
HackMaster	Enhancement	Loading and management of system hacks to modify PalmPilot behavior.
HandStamp	E-mail/Terminal	Full-featured PPP e-mail.
Hangman	Entertainment	Electronic version of the pen-and-paper game.
Hourz	Productivity	Track your time for billing purposes.
HushHack	Enhancement	Disables the HotSync tones.
Jump	Programming	Java-like programming for the PalmPilot.
Klondike	Entertainment	PalmPilot version the card game
Launch Pad	Enhancement	Replacement Application Launcher with multiple pages for categorizing applications.
LoanCalc	Financial	Calculate loan payment schedules.

Online Source	Memory Required	On the CD?
www.dovcom.com/	8K	✓
www.electronhut.com/pilot/	16K	✓
www.usr.com/palm/software.html	18K, 9K, 4K, 18K	
www.mindspring.com/~jetton/pilot/ index.html	14K	✓
cpu563.adsl.sympatico.ca/gcm.htm	n/a	
www.electronhut.com/pilot/	5K	✓
home1.pacific.net.sg/~kokmun/ pilotpgm.htm	21K	✓
www.1stresource.com/~mistered/ hackmstr.htm	10K	
www.smartcodesoft.com/	63K	✓
www.gate.net/~dhaupert/ ddhpilot.html	27K	✓
www.best.com/~zaeske/ zoskware.shtml	31K	
www.mindspring.com/~jetton/ pilot/index.html	3K	✓
userzweb.lightspeed.net/~gregh/ pilot/jump/index.html	n/a	
www.electronhut.com/pilot/	18K	✓
www.nwlink.com/~emilyk/ LaunchPad/	23K	
www.csun.edu/~hbcsc274/	23K	

continues

continued

App Name	Category	Description
LookAtMe	Clock	Sets alarms to trigger specific applications at time(s) specified.
MakeDoc	Electronic Text & Utils	Conversion utility for creating DOC files.
MakeDoc for Windows	Electronic Text & Utils	Windows conversion utility for creating DOC files.
MathPad	Calculator	Equation solver.
MetriCalc	Calculator	Calculator with metric conversions.
Missile Command	Entertainment	Arcade game for PalmPilot, modeled after the Atari game by the same name.
MoneyCalc	Financial	Several calculation routines for various financial operations. (requires cbasPad)
Morse Code	Entertainment	Practice your Morse code.
MusicBox	Entertainment	Compose and play music on PalmPilot (requires cbasPad).
Online	E-mail/Terminal	VT-100 terminal emulator.
Operating System Upgrades	Upgrade	Upgrades various PalmPilot Operating Systems.
Outliner	Productivity	Create outlines with a multi-tude of features.
PalmDraw	Graphics	Full-featured vector object-drawing program.
Palmeta Mail	E-mail/Terminal	Conduit to send and receive e-mail via the Memo Pad.
PaperClip	Programming	Utility to perform a hard reset.
Pegged	Entertainment	Jump the pegs to leave only one left.

Online Source	Memory Required	On the CD?
Home.InfoRamp.Net/~adam/pilot	10K	✓
www.corel.com/people/patb.htm	n/a	
ourworld.compuserve.com/homepages/Mark_Pierce/	n/a	✓
www.probe.net/~rhuebner/mathpad.html	32K	✓
198.70.114.128/stinger/stingersoft.cfm	14K	✓
www.contrib.andrew.cmu.edu/usr/galahad/	15K	
home1.pacific.net.sg/~kokmun/basic.htm	8K	✓
www-cs-students.stanford.edu/~echeng/Pilot/pilot.html	4K	
home1.pacific.net.sg/~kokmun/basic.htm	2K	✓
www.hausofmaus.com	19K	✓
www.usr.com/palm	Varies	
w3.teaser.fr/~fpillet/pilot/outliner.html	57K	✓
www.oai.com/bkg/Pilot/PalmDraw/	40K	
www.palmeta.com	n/a	✓
www.mindspring.com/~jetton/pilot/index.html	1K	✓
home1.pacific.net.sg/~kokmun/pilotpgm.htm	18K	✓

continues

continued

App Name	Category	Description
Perplex	Entertainment	Slide the blocks to relocate the large block in the shortest number of moves.
PhotoAlbum	Graphics	Display grayscale images on PalmPilot. (Demo)
Pikoban	Entertainment	Push boxes around a maze to their destination.
PilA	Programming	Create PalmPilot resource files (PRC) from 68000 assembly code.
Pilot App Launcher	Enhancement	Replacement Application Launcher with multiple categories for apps.
Pilot DOC	Electronic Text & Utils	Large document display.
Pilot Forms	Productivity	Create graphical interface forms for data collection. (demo)
Pilot Mail MAPI	E-mail/Terminal	Link PalmPilot to your MAPI-compatible e-mail client.
PilotMoney Exporter	Financial	Export PilotMoney data to the desktop.
Pilot Secrets	Enhancement	Encrypts and decrypts PalmPilot data.
PilotClock 1.0 (demo)	Clock	Clock with stopwatch and timer capabilities. (demo)
PilotMoney Suite	Financial	Keep track of multiple accounts on your PalmPilot.
PilRC	Programming	PalmPilot resource compiler.
PocketSynth	Entertainment	Play music on PalmPilot.

Online Source	Memory Required	On the CD?
www.dovcom.com/	8K	✓
members.aol.com/PilotPhoto/	34K	✓
home1.pacific.net.sg/~kokmun/pilotpgm.htm	31K	✓
www.massena.com/darrin/pilot/tanda.htm	n/a	
www.dovcom.com/	19K	✓
www.concentric.net/~rbram/doc.shtml	25K	✓
www.webfayre.com/pilot	80K	
www.algonet.se/~fth/Pilot/	n/a	
198.70.114.128/stinger/stingersoft.cfm	10K	
www.followme.com/abastien/encrypt.html	12K	
www.LWSD.com/	31K	✓
198.70.114.128/stinger/stingersoft.cfm	35K (OS1), 34K (OS2)	✓
www.scumby.com/scumbysoft/pilot/pilrc/index.htm	n/a	
www-cs-students.stanford.edu/~echeng/Pilot/pilot.html	16K	✓

continues

continued

App Name	Category	Description
PostCalc	Calculator	Postage calculator.
Power Hack	Enhancement	Companion for CheckIn, provides automatic locking the PalmPilot is powered off.
PV Poker	Entertainment	PalmPilot version of Video Poker.
QDraw	Graphics	A vector-based object drawing program.
QPaint	Graphics	Full-featured bitmap drawing program.
QMate	Financial	Import/export Quicken data.
QuickSheet	Spreadsheet	A full-featured spreadsheet for your PalmPilot (commercial only).
ReDo	Productivity	Schedule recurring reminders for to-do lists.
Reptoids	Entertainment	Asteroid-like game.
Reversi	Entertainment	Classic board game for PalmPilot.
RipCord	PC Utilities	Performs full backup and restore of PalmPilot data.
RollEm	Entertainment	Dice simulator.
RPN	Calculator	Reverse Polish Notation calculator with powerful scripting capability.
Scratch Pad	Graphics	Draw simple freehand figures.
Scribble	Graphics	Draw simple freehand figures.
Secret	Enhancement	Encryption for Memo Pad.
SilentAppInstaller	PC Utilities	Installs applications.

Online Source	Memory Required	On the CD?
www.dovcom.com/	4K	✓
dialspace.dial.pipex.com/town/parade/aag02/pilot	2K	✓
web2.airmail.net/mike2me/Pilot	25K	
www.t3.rim.or.jp/quanta/English	19K	✓
www.t3.rim.or.jp/~quanta/English	13K	✓
www.wco.com/~johnr/steve/qmate.html	32K	✓
www.cesinc.com/products.asp	135K	
http://www.probe.net/~rhuebner/redo.html	37K	✓
Home.InfoRamp.Net/~adam/pilot/about/23.html	31K	
Home.InfoRamp.Net/~adam/pilot/about/11.html	7K	
wr.com.au/harryo/ripcord/	n/a	
www.ms.uky.edu/~kilroy/pilot/	2K	
fatmac.ee.cornell.edu/~rwebb/pilot.html	34K	✓
Home.InfoRamp.Net/~adam/pilot	5K	
www.iosphere.net/~howlett/pilot/	3K	
www.tphys.uni-heidelberg.de/~linke/pilot/	8K	✓
ucsub.colorado.edu/~eilebrec/saip/saip.html	n/a	✓

continues

continued

App Name	Category	Description
SilkHack	Enhancement	Redefine silkscreen buttons.
SimpleTerm	E-mail/Terminal	A simple ASCII terminal.
SlimCalc Upgrade/Patch (USR)	Upgrade	Upgrade for original Pilot 1000 Calculator.
Space Invaders	Entertainment	Arcade game for PalmPilot, modeled after the Atari game by the same name.
StingerMail	E-mail/Terminal	Enhanced interface for Palmeta Mail.
Sums	Calculator	Utility for keeping lists of numbers and their totals.
SuperPad	Text Editor	A super Memo Pad editor.
TimeReporter	Productivity	Track your time for billing purposes.
TransAOL	E-mail/Terminal	Read your America Online e-mail on PalmPilot.
Tricorder	Entertainment	Scan for life forms and operate other amusing functions.
VolumeControl	Enhancement	Change the tone of multiple PalmPilot sounds.
Wheel of Fortune	Entertainment	Just like the game show of the same name.
Windows Icon Editor	Programming	Create and edit PalmPilot icons for applications.
WorldTime	Clock	Displays the time for locations around the world.
ymCal	Calendar	Shows monthly view of appointments and To Do items.
ymFrag	Enhancement	Helps defragment the PalmPilot's memory.

Online Source	Memory Required	On the CD?
198.70.114.128/stinger/stingersoft.cfm	7K	✓
www.hausofmaus.com	8K	✓
www.usr.com/palm/custsupp/upgrade.html	17K	
www.eskimo.com/~scottlu/pilot/	9K	
198.70.114.128/stinger/stingersoft.cfm	18K	
www.tphys.uni-heidelberg.de/~linke/pilot/sums.html	15K	✓
ahinds.vip.best.com/~ahinds/	27K	
www.iambic.com	???	✓
members.aol.com/vincedeb/index.html	n/a	
www.mindspring.com/~jetton/pilot/index.html	9K	✓
home.pacific.net.sg/~kokmun/basic.htm	7K	✓
www.jaegertech.com/jtwof/default.htm	23K	
www.oai.com/bkg/Pilot/	n/a	
Home.InfoRamp.Net/~adam/pilot/	10K	✓
www.nicholson.com/rhn/pilot.html	15K	
www.nicholson.com/rhn/pilot.html		

Index

Symbols

A

H

I

J-K

L

M-N

Q-R

U-V

W-X-Y-Z

Complete and Return this Card for a *FREE* Computer Book Catalog

Thank you for purchasing this book! You have purchased a superior computer book written expressly for your needs. To continue to provide the kind of up-to-date, pertinent coverage you've come to expect from us, we need to hear from you. Please take a minute to complete and return this self-addressed, postage-paid form. In return, we'll send you a free catalog of all our computer books on topics ranging from word processing to programming and the internet.

Mr. ☐ Mrs. ☐ Ms. ☐ Dr. ☐

Name (first) ☐☐☐☐☐☐☐☐☐☐☐ (M.I.) ☐ (last) ☐☐☐☐☐☐☐☐☐☐☐☐☐☐☐

Address ☐☐☐☐☐☐☐☐☐☐☐☐☐☐☐☐☐☐☐☐☐☐☐☐☐☐☐☐☐☐☐☐☐☐☐

☐☐☐☐☐☐☐☐☐☐☐☐☐☐☐☐☐☐☐☐☐☐☐☐☐☐☐☐☐☐☐☐☐☐☐

City ☐☐☐☐☐☐☐☐☐☐☐☐☐☐☐ State ☐☐ Zip ☐☐☐☐☐ ☐☐☐☐☐

Phone ☐☐☐ ☐☐☐ ☐☐☐☐ Fax ☐☐☐ ☐☐☐ ☐☐☐☐

Company Name ☐☐☐☐☐☐☐☐☐☐☐☐☐☐☐☐☐☐☐☐☐☐☐☐☐☐☐☐☐☐☐☐☐

E-mail address ☐☐☐☐☐☐☐☐☐☐☐☐☐☐☐☐☐☐☐☐☐☐☐☐☐☐☐☐☐☐☐☐☐

1. Please check at least (3) influencing factors for purchasing this book.

- Front or back cover information on book .... ☐
- Special approach to the content .... ☐
- Completeness of content .... ☐
- Author's reputation .... ☐
- Publisher's reputation .... ☐
- Book cover design or layout .... ☐
- Index or table of contents of book .... ☐
- Price of book .... ☐
- Special effects, graphics, illustrations .... ☐
- Other (Please specify): ______________ ☐

2. How did you first learn about this book?

- Internet Site .... ☐
- Saw in Macmillan Computer Publishing catalog .... ☐
- Recommended by store personnel .... ☐
- Saw the book on bookshelf at store .... ☐
- Recommended by a friend .... ☐
- Received advertisement in the mail .... ☐
- Saw an advertisement in: ______________ ☐
- Read book review in: ______________ ☐
- Other (Please specify): ______________ ☐

3. How many computer books have you purchased in the last six months?

- This book only .... ☐
- 3 to 5 books .... ☐
- 2 books .... ☐
- More than 5 .... ☐

4. Where did you purchase this book?

- Bookstore .... ☐
- Computer Store .... ☐
- Consumer Electronics Store .... ☐
- Department Store .... ☐
- Office Club .... ☐
- Warehouse Club .... ☐
- Mail Order .... ☐
- Direct from Publisher .... ☐
- Internet site .... ☐
- Other (Please specify): .... ☐

5. How long have you been using a computer?

- Less than 6 months .. ☐
- 6 months to a year ..... ☐
- 1 to 3 years .... ☐
- More than 3 years ...... ☐

6. What is your level of experience with personal computers and with the subject of this book?

	With PC's	With subject of book
New	☐	☐
Casual	☐	☐
Accomplished	☐	☐
Expert	☐	☐

Source Code — ISBN: 0-7897-1248-2

7. Which of the following best describes your job title?

Administrative Assistant ☐
Coordinator ☐
Manager/Supervisor ☐
Director ☐
Vice President ☐
President/CEO/COO ☐
Lawyer/Doctor/Medical Professional ☐
Teacher/Educator/Trainer ☐
Engineer/Technician ☐
Consultant ☐
Not employed/Student/Retired ☐
Other (Please specify): ☐

8. Which of the following best describes the area of the company your job title falls under?

Accounting ☐
Engineering ☐
Manufacturing ☐
Marketing ☐
Operations ☐
Sales ☐
Other (Please specify): ☐

9. What is your age?

Under 20 ☐
21-29 ☐
30-39 ☐
40-49 ☐
50-59 ☐
60-over ☐

10. Are you:

Male ☐
Female ☐

11. Which computer publications do you read regularly? (Please list)

____

____

____

____

____

____

____

____

____

Comments: ______________________________

____

____

Fold here and scotch-tape to mail.

NO POSTAGE NECESSARY IF MAILED IN THE UNITED STATES

BUSINESS REPLY MAIL

FIRST-CLASS MAIL PERMIT NO. 9918 INDIANAPOLIS IN

POSTAGE WILL BE PAID BY THE ADDRESSEE

ATTN MARKETING
MACMILLAN COMPUTER PUBLISHING
MACMILLAN PUBLISHING USA
201 W 103RD ST
INDIANAPOLIS IN 46290-9042

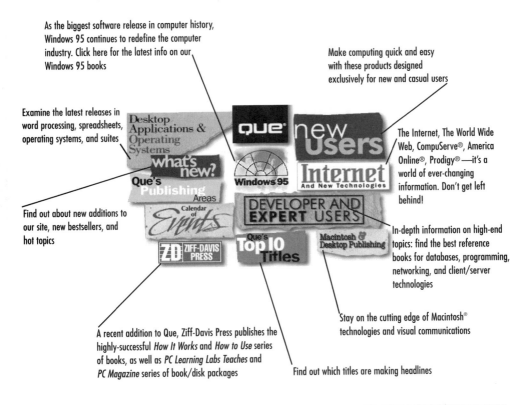

Read This Before Opening Software

By opening this package, you are agreeing to be bound by the following:

The software on this CD-ROM for *Pilot Companion* is copyrighted and all rights are reserved by the publisher and its licensors. You are licensed to use this software on a single computer and single Pilot. You may copy the software for backup or archival purposes only. Making copies of the software for any other purpose is a violation of United States copyright laws. THIS SOFTWARE IS SOLD AS IS, WITHOUT WARRANTY OF ANY KIND, EITHER EXPRESS OR IMPLIED, INCLUDING BUT NOT LIMITED TO THE IMPLIED WARRANTIES OF MERCHANABILITY AND FITNESS FOR A PARTICULAR PURPOSE. Neither the publisher, nor its dealers and distributors, nor its licensors assume any liability for any alleged or actual damages arising from the use of this software. (Some states do not allow exclusion of implied warranties, so the exclusion may not apply to you.)

The entire contents of this CD-ROM and the compilation of the software are copyrighted and protected by United States copyright laws. The individual programs on the CD-ROM are copyrighted by the authors or owners of each program. Each program has its own use permissions and limitations. To use each program, you must follow the individual requirements and restrictions detailed for each. Do not use a program if you do not agree to follow its licensing agreement.